Behind the Lights, the Tote and the Non-starters

A look at the welfare of greyhounds bred for racing in Britain and the campaigns and debate surrounding their treatment

Sighthoundmad

Published by Grey UK
greyuk@outlook.com
ISBN 978-0-9928394-0-6

Contents

Contents: tables

Contents: images

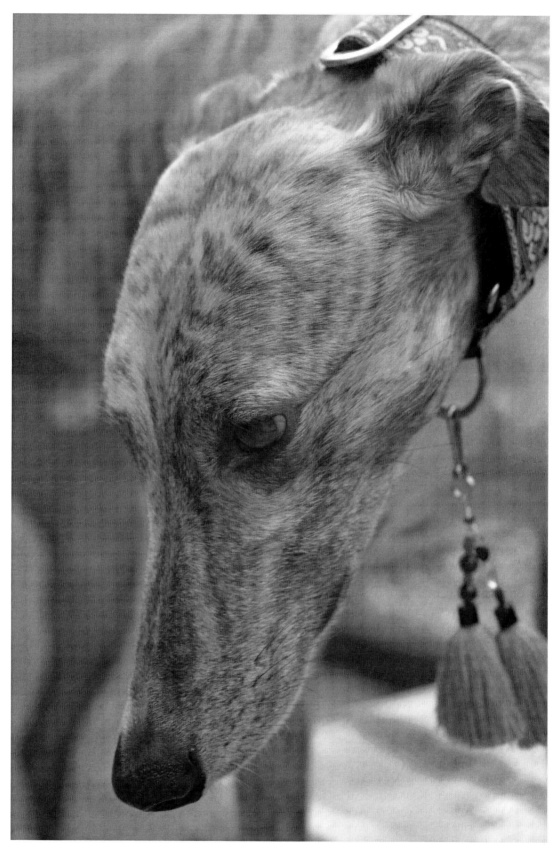

Jake: retired from racing after suffering a hock fracture in only his seventh race.
Fractures of the hock are one of the more common career-ending injuries and though
treatable, invariably result in the greyhound being put down (on economical grounds)

1

Introduction

It is a cold December evening and I am heading to Yarmouth greyhound stadium to join a group of people demonstrating outside the track. It will be my first meeting with any of the protesters and the first demonstration I have taken part in and what I am not is an anarchist or tree-hugging hippy but rather just someone who cares passionately about greyhounds.

For as long as I can remember I have been fond of animals and the barking variety in particular. As a child there was always a spaniel sticking a wet nose in my face but not until the late eighties and many years after leaving the parental nest did I consider adoption myself. A local rescue had in mind one dog in particular as suitable for my circumstances: a small, young mongrel, ginger in colour and admittedly very sweet but not the one for me. I was shown the others and my attention was immediately drawn to a beautiful light brindle bitch called Rosie. She was a greyhound or greyhound cross, perhaps eight or nine years old and over-looked by everyone, likely because of her age.

Rosie would not be over-looked any more and was to prove the most affectionate and adorable animal you could possibly imagine, though sadly our time together was short lived as within two years Rosie became very ill and I was to lose her. Those two years, however, will stay with me forever and proved life-changing. Becky followed - a dark brindle one-year-old greyhound and dare I say a little under weight. Although from the same kennels as Rosie, Becky was not strictly speaking a rescue dog. Her mother was picked up as a stray in Workington and found to be pregnant and Becky was the last of a litter of seven puppies to be found a home.

Close to the rescue was a greyhound track but I never linked the story of either Becky or Rosie to greyhound racing. I never gave it any thought and had no interest in racing. I naïvely assumed that a dog running on a track was foremost a pet and viewed and treated in the way you would hope a pet dog is viewed and treated. The racing industry would certainly like you to think that.

Much has changed in my life since the late eighties but the one constant has been the company of a greyhound or should I say greyhounds. One became two and if it was not for the financial and practical issues I would likely now have a house full of greyhounds. Two is a sensible, manageable number, importantly two can be controlled independently when taken for a walk and I have learnt that a boy and girl is the ideal partnership.

I remained utterly ignorant about the welfare issues associated with the breed and that would perhaps still be the case today if not for the internet, and being a member of the older generation this was technology resisted for many years. Not until 2002 was I online and not until a few years later did I stumble across the site for Greyhound Action (GA) detailing a catalogue of cruelty to racing dogs. GA was ultimately seeking an end to commercial greyhound racing. The group would argue, as indeed I have since done, that commercial greyhound racing and the humane treatment of greyhounds is incompatible.

Across Britain there were both individuals and groups - some using the GA name, some using their own name - supporting the cause and local to me was Norwich-based Action for Greyhounds (AFG). This group would occasionally hold demonstrations outside Yarmouth greyhound stadium, and with the above providing an opportunity to get involved so it was back in December 2006 I found myself holding a 'running for their lives' placard to all race-goers entering the stadium.

In the years since I have supported AFG in various ways though primarily worked independently on research. Campaign groups covered the basics and focused largely on the dogs' ultimate fate. I wanted a better understanding on numbers and to explore in detail key welfare issues. Besides which I'm one of those difficult people compelled to question everything and a firm believer in evidence-based research - something lacking in the claims made by antis. The outcome has broadened the welfare debate and ruffled a few feathers - both amongst members of the racing fraternity and those who oppose racing - but for me there was never an agenda bar simply reporting and formulating opinion on what I found.

The facts and figures associated with racing dogs are endless and in the last six years I have collated many of them. Two surveys undertaken are the largest of their kind: the first establishing the percentage of British registered puppies making the grade to race and the second looking at racing results in relation to injuries. Injuries is a subject I keep coming back to and it is without question the most sensitive issue for racings' officials.

Much information can be gained through a variety of publications and the internet but it was the numerous conversations I had with members of the racing fraternity to include more than one hundred trainers that were particularly enlightening... and not always in ways you might think. Many were hostile, suspicious or guarded and none more so than the partner of trainer Joy Andrews (attached to Belle Vue, Manchester) who, when asked merely about the welfare of one particular dog, threatened to kick my "fucking" head in.[1-1] Welcome to the world of greyhound racing.

In the last six years the industry has reinvented itself. Damaging media coverage and a fall in popularity meant it had to or there would likely not be an industry for much longer, but in reality little has changed for the dogs. And in the last six years I have lost all faith in the RSPCA. In theory there is legislation in place that should protect greyhounds, in reality it is hardly worth the paper it is written on, and for reasons not clear the charity is not pushing for measures that would all but eliminate wide-spread abuse and suffering of dogs bred for racing. The Scottish SPCA is no better.

The fall in popularity has though dictated a fall in the number of greyhounds bred and thus a fall in the number of greyhounds unaccounted for and presumed killed. GA can take some credit for this but a national co-ordinated campaign opposing commercial racing has now fragmented. The writing was perhaps on the wall when 'supporter' Trudy Baker got involved and I find myself increasingly questioning the mindset and actions of many supporting the cause. I could never though question their fundamental objective. Antis want to protect greyhounds and expose the truth whereas industry officials want to protect the business of greyhound racing and conceal the truth, and like it or hate it, the industry is today enjoying smoother waters.

This publication offers a unique insight into opposing camps, and details the key welfare issues associated with dogs bred for racing in Britain to include the most comprehensive and up-to-date figures on greyhounds unaccounted for. It further offers an independent perspective on the welfare debate and ultimately cuts through much of the rhetoric I have digested in the last six years. My obvious passion for greyhounds extends also into photography, and accompanying images of greyhounds as pets are selections from my own ever-increasing library.

Lulu: contended over 150 races and had her seasons suppressed so she could be earning run-money every month. The brindle bitch survived the racing without serious injury but her behaviour when first adopted would indicate she was treated harshly

2

A brief history of the racing industry

The concept of greyhound racing as we know it today originates from America and was made possible with Owen Patrick Smith's design for a mechanical hare or lure. The idea of a lure in greyhound racing was being tested as early as the 1870s in England but significantly Smith perfected a system to work on a circular course. Some eight years later in 1920 the first meeting on a purpose built circular race track took place at Emeryville, California.

Not long afterwards entrepreneur Charles Munn bought the overseas rights for the patented hare and in 1925 formed the Greyhound Racing Association (GRA) with three British partners: coursing trainer and judge Major Lyne Dixson; former Chief Constable of Brighton, Sir William Gentle, and Brigadier-General Alfred Cecil Critchley.

The Association secured a seven-year lease on a site belonging to the adjacent Belle Vue zoological gardens and on 24 July 1926 the first race meeting in Britain was staged. Mistley won the opening race, contended by seven runners over a quarter-mile distance. The meeting had its problems, not least with the mechanical lure, and lost money but attendances quickly rose and the company was in a position to repay a bank loan of £10,000 before the end of the first season in October.

There are wildly conflicting reports on how many tracks were in operation by the end of the following year with a figure of 30 at the lower end of the scale. Certainly, however, greyhound racing had very quickly become a national phenomenon. The centrepiece for the GRA was White City in London; a stadium that was originally built for the 1908 Olympic Games. Now very tired-looking it was revamped for greyhound meetings and doors opened to race-goers on 20 June 1927. The following month White City staged the first Greyhound Derby with Entry Badge claiming the £1,000 winner's prize.

The Derby - the most prestigious of all greyhound races - stayed at White City until the track was demolished in 1984, and from 1985 onwards Wimbledon became the host track.

Promoters early on recognised a need to have public confidence in racing. So it was in January 1928 the National Greyhound Racing Club (NGRC) came into being as the rule-making judiciary body. The 'sport' gained a further institution - the British Greyhound Racing Board (BGRB) (that would ultimately adopt in all but name a governing role) - when recommendations of a special working party were approved at a meeting in April 1979. The meeting further approved the establishment of a new trade association, the NGRC Licensed Racecourse Promoters Association (RCPA).

Key in the development and success of greyhound racing was the use of the totalisator; a relatively new invention providing an automated 'pool' system of track betting. The GRA-owned Harringay Park was one of the first stadiums to install such a machine in 1930 but it was to prove controversial both from a legal point of view and, not surprisingly, with bookmakers. The matter was resolved at least in part when the tote was legalised under the Betting and Lotteries Act 1934.

Within 10 years of Mistley winning the first race, annual attendances at NGRC tracks alone had risen to 25 million and in the early post war years the figure reached 50 million. While the latter figure (given in a NGRC Calendar supplement) is questionably high, annual turnover on totalisators speaks for itself: £39 million in 1938 rising to £75 million in 1944. Peacetime conditions saw the figure increase from £138 million in 1945 to £200 million in 1946.

The 'sport' was benefiting from increased disposable wealth and limited spending opportunities but with gambling such an integral part of greyhound racing wrong-doing was rife and emotions ran high. At Harringay in July 1946 the disqualification of a well-supported dog provoked a riot. Starting traps were burned, the restaurant, press box and totalisator were targeted - with money reportedly being grabbed - and both track officials and police reinforcement were attacked.

On 31 July 1946 the Daily Herald reported that former Chief Constable Percy Worth was to head the newly-formed Greyhound Race Tracks Security Police intended "to chase dog-dopers, tote-ticket forgers, the 'beat-up' men and rowdies from the tracks." Any prestige the industry had enjoyed was fast being eroded. According to the London Times one Labour MP went so far as to say "most people concerned with greyhound racing are social parasites."[2-1]

The government carried little favour with the industry at the time and when faced with an energy crisis early in 1947 a ban was imposed on greyhound racing as a fuel-saving measure. It was short lived but affected 1,200 races. A restriction on mid-week fixtures was then imposed in a bid to counter absenteeism from work and remained in place, albeit with an easing from April 1948, until 1949. Most damaging was a 10 percent levy on the money wagered using dog totalisators as part of the last budget by Chancellor Hugh Dalton in November 1947.

From a post-war peak greyhound racing was losing favour also with the public. Attendances across larger tracks fell in the region of 40 percent by 1950 and totalisator takings for the same year had more than halved to £72 million. By 1960 the takings were down a further £10 million and the slide continued with the legalisation of betting offices in 1961.

The response from the industry was a 'Smash the Tax' campaign. According to Archie Newhouse, recollecting his time as editor with the Greyhound Express, "it gathered tremendous support in the media, on television and in the regional and national newspapers, [...] and I was running a round-the-clock control centre from our offices in Fleet Street, sending out press releases."[2-2] It culminated in the delivery of a 100,000 signatures' petition to the House of Commons but the government response was to increase the levy to 11 percent.

Participating tracks did, however, benefit from a new income with the Bookmakers Afternoon Greyhound Service (BAGS), established in 1967. It was born out of a desire on the part of bookies to offer clients an alternative betting product when horse racing was cancelled due to bad weather. From humble beginnings the BAGS service now accounts for virtually all off-course betting turnover generated through greyhound racing.

Further, in 1992 a new measure was introduced that would provide funding for the regulated side of the industry by way of a levy of 0.25 percent of bookmakers turnover on greyhound racing. It was the beginning of the British Greyhound Racing Fund (BGRF) and the levy was increased to 0.4 percent in 1996 and 0.6 percent in 2006 but it was, and remains, only a voluntary levy and a number of bookmakers (accounting for about 17 percent of turnover in 2007) do not contribute.

With the levy based on betting turnover and that turnover derived almost entirely from BAGS coverage, and with a situation nowadays where the majority of regulated tracks receive an income from much sought-after BAGS contracts (an estimated £26m spilt between 18 tracks in 2012), it cannot be overstated how important BAGS is to commercial greyhound racing in Britain. It should though also be noted that BAGS meetings accounted for only about one third of races staged in more recent years by tracks eligible to bid for such contracts.

Be it on-course or off-course the real attraction in greyhound racing is betting. The dogs therefore act primarily as a betting medium and are viewed as a commodity and this was, and is, reflected in their treatment. Towards the end of the twentieth century their welfare has, however, gathered increasing public, political, media and charity scrutiny, and ever increasing negative publicity has shook the industry to its very core.

Pioneers in finding homes for retired greyhounds include Ann Shannon, who was involved in their rescue as far back as the late fifties, and Johanna Beumer, awarded the MBE in 2007 for services to greyhound welfare and, more specifically, her work in rescuing ex-Walthamstow dogs from 1965 onwards. In 1974 a number of homing schemes were brought together under one umbrella called the NGRC Retired Greyhound Trust but industry funding to help ex-racers was minimal and the number of greyhounds adopted annually was pitifully low compared against breeding figures.

The BBC On the Line documentary "Cradle to grave," aired in January 1994, uncovered "the often brutal reality behind an industry which destroys up to 30,000 dogs a year." The programme instigated a debate the following month in the House of Commons on cruelty to greyhounds, and growing public awareness about their treatment and fate led to the formation of a number of greyhound protection groups in the nineties, including perhaps the best-known GA in 1997.

It took, however, the exposure in July 2006 of builders' merchant David Smith killing racing dogs on an industrial scale for parliament, if not the industry, to give greyhound welfare the attention it warranted. The Sunday Times article detailing how Smith was paid £10 a time to use a bolt gun on the dogs was to result in the Associate Parliamentary Group for Animal Welfare (APGAW) conducting a six-month inquiry into the welfare of racing dogs in England.

The industry response was to commission an 'independent' review of regulation, chaired by Lord Donoughue of Ashton.[2-3] Recommendations within led to changes in the structure of the regulatory and governing authority that came into effect, officially, on 1 January 2009 when a new body - the Greyhound Board of Great Britain (GBGB) - took over the roles of the NGRC and BGRB. Many old personnel remained.

Better protection for racing dogs in the form of statutory legislation came on the back of the Animal Welfare Act 2006 when, on 6 April 2010, the Welfare of Racing Greyhounds Regulations 2010 came into effect. It went some way to bring the independent tracks in line with tracks governed by the GBGB, and though strongly criticised by all welfare groups for being too limited it contains one essential requirement; the attendance of a veterinary surgeon at all races, trials and sales trials.

In 2013 and following a challenging decade the industry has reached arguably a more sustainable size. At the time of writing there are 25 tracks regulated by the GBGB and race meetings being staged on a regular basis at 10 independent venues, compared with a track total exceeding 220 in the 'sports' heyday. Annual attendances have fallen to a little above two million.

History of NGRC tracks

Tracks operational under the NGRC and now defunct

Aberdeen Holborn	Hull Holderness Road	Norwich Boundary Park
Birmingham Kings Heath	Ipswich	Norwich City
Birmingham Perry Barr (old)	Leeds	Nottingham White City
Blackpool	Leicester	Oxford
Bolton	Liverpool Breck	Plymouth
Bournemouth	Liverpool Seaforth	Portsmouth
Bradford City	Liverpool Stanley	Preston
Bradford Greenfield	Liverpool White City	Ramsgate
Bristol Eastville	London Catford	Rayleigh

Bristol Knowle

Burnley

Cambridge

Canterbury

Cardiff

Cardiff White City

Clacton

Cradley Heath

Dagenham

Derby

Dundee

Edinburgh Powderhall

Edinburgh Stenhouse

Exeter

Falkirk

Gateshead

Glasgow Albion

Glasgow Carntyne

Glasgow Firhill

Glasgow White City

Gloucester

Halifax

Hull Boulevard

London Charlton

London Clapton

London Hackney

London Harringay

London Hendon

London New Cross

London Park Royal

London Stamford Bridge

London Walthamstow

London Wandsworth

London Wembley

London West Ham

London White City

Long Eaton

Maidstone

Manchester White City

Mansfield

Middlesbrough

Milton Keynes

Newcastle Gosforth

Newcastle White City

Newport

Norton Canes

Reading

Reading (old)

Rochdale

Rochester

Rye House

Salford

Sheffield Darnall

Slough

Southampton

Southend

South Shields

Spennymoor

Stanley

Stoke

Sunderland (old)

Swaffham

Tamworth

Wakefield

Warrington

Watford

Whitwood

Wisbech

Wolverhampton Willenhall

Open and now regulated under the GBGB

Birmingham Hall Green

Birmingham Perry Barr

Brighton & Hove

Coventry

Crayford

Doncaster

Glasgow Shawfield

Harlow

Henlow

Kinsley

London Wimbledon

Manchester Belle Vue

Mildenhall

Newcastle Brough Park

Nottingham

Pelaw Grange

Peterborough

Poole

Romford

Sheffield Owlerton

Sittingbourne

Sunderland

Swindon

Wolverhampton Monmore

Yarmouth

Annual race totals across 2008-12

	2008	2009	2010	2011	2012
Belle Vue	3356	2883	2715	2781	2643
Brough Park	3399	3359	3355	3368	3279
Coventry	1757	1561	nil	nil	780
Crayford	3383	3289	3235	3308	3217
Doncaster	1418	1312	1019	960	993
Hall Green	3341	3256	3165	3040	2563
Harlow	2015	1824	1623	1293	1024
Henlow	1739	1780	1797	1695	1707
Hove	3538	3601	3150	3196	3204
Hull	1091	437	nil	nil	nil
Kinsley	2058	2418	2323	2357	2494
Mildenhall	1192	1112	898	960	885
Monmore	2791	2805	2801	2765	2802
Nottingham	2935	2891	2901	2884	2888
Owlerton	3581	3530	3560	3599	3628
Oxford	3071	2553	2519	2578	2275
Pelaw Grange	1569	1521	1460	1573	1455
Perry Barr	3099	2528	2484	2450	2358
Peterborough	2652	2109	2133	2144	2156
Poole	1957	1976	1935	1998	1922
Portsmouth	1843	1712	266	nil	nil
Reading	1410	nil	nil	nil	nil
Romford	4121	3997	3989	4016	4017
Shawfield	1576	1581	1533	1320	1125
Sittingbourne	2016	1981	1786	1962	1985
Sunderland	3350	3375	3205	3288	3263
Swindon	3288	3172	3217	3163	3112
Walthamstow	2032	nil	nil	nil	nil
Wimbledon	1995	1884	1391	1469	1283
Yarmouth	2072	2090	1954	2034	2042

The table highlights six tracks that across the above time period closed for business though with Coventry opening once again in May 2012 (Oxford ceased operating on 29 December 2012). It also identifies a significant fall in races held for other tracks, notably Belle Vue, Hall Green, Perry Barr, Wimbledon and, in particular, Harlow where figures are down by almost half.[2-4]

THE GREYHOUND RACING ASSOCIATION
(MANCHESTER) LTD.

BELLE VUE TRACK
GORTON, MANCHESTER

Racing every Monday, Wednesday and Saturday

at 7.30 p.m.

Covered Stands, Seating Accommodation,

and Refreshment Rooms in all enclosures.

CAR PARKS UNDER SUPERVISION OF THE R.A.C.

Telephone　　:　　:　　:　　:　　　OPENSHAW 900 and 901.

Telegrams　　:　　:　　:　　　RACINGREYS, MANCHESTER.

Advertisement featured in The National Greyhound Racing Calendar,
4 April 1928

3

The modern trainer

In a one page fanciful article (courtesy of Our Dogs) Greyhound Star editor Floyd Amphlett conjured up a romantic image of greyhound racing that had little in common with reality. "You build a kennel," writes Amphlett, "buy a greyhound, pay for its registrations, inoculations and the rest, apply for a licence and then race at your closest track. It is a hobby not so different to those of you readers of Our Dogs who enjoy agility training, fly-ball, or other assorted fun activities with dogs."[3-1]

Theoretically you could have a greyhound timed at one of the independent tracks (commonly referred to as flapping tracks) and the dog could, the following week, be contesting a race. And due to plummeting prize money and rising costs it might be reasonable to assume the hobby trainer is just what the 'sport' needs but 'one man and his dog' cannot be accommodated for by the dominant regulated sector of greyhound racing that is increasingly dependent on professional trainers.

To be fair to Amphlett his article served to counter much 'anti material' previously published by Our Dogs and was in effect a free promotional opportunity for the racing industry and not something that could be taken as a serious piece of journalism. A kennel strength of 50 or 100 or more is not uncommon nowadays with trainers contracted to supply 'x' number of dogs to a track where the racing manager is under huge pressure to fill race cards. Small trainers are being pushed out and the bigger players are fighting to keep their heads above water.

All trainers registered with the GBGB are listed on the group website and the total recorded was 1,248, 1,151, 981 and 883 in January 2009, 2010, 2011 and 2012, respectively. In percentage terms the dramatic decline is greater than the fall in the number of races held for the same period, as might be expected where the non-professional category (restricted to 12 greyhounds) account for many leaving the 'sport'.

Trainers quitting in late 2011 included David Bull and Steve King. For Nottingham trainer Bull, veterinary bills and ever increasing costs for materials, diesel and feed were making it very difficult to replace dogs lost through injury and 'old' age. His kennel strength dropped from 38 at its peak to 18. King moved to Poole when Portsmouth closed but with owners not getting enough runs to make it worthwhile, decided Swindon would be a better option. His outgoings exceeded £1,200 per month on rent, business and water rates alone, and working up to 80 hours a week to just survive was for King the end.

Reduced prize money is seeing also a massive decline in owners. It is a sector of the racing fraternity rarely appreciated by tracks but when greyhounds are not paying their way, having the kennel fees covered by an owner or syndicate can be the difference between breaking even and going under. It is, however, a double-edged sword with many owners refusing to meet their financial obligations and not taking responsibility for dogs of no further use or value.

It's a far cry from the image conjured up by Amphlett, and to succeed in the 'sport' nowadays a factory-like operation is required; an operation of the kind that inevitably impacts on the well-being and welfare of the animals. Longtime breeder, trainer and owner Brian King is on record saying:

> I deal with quite a few professional kennels in England and in my opinion very few dogs are actually trained, most are just handled. I don't blame the trainers. They have to have so many dogs in the kennel to make ends meet that they simply don't get the time. […] it is impossible for anyone to handle more than 10 dogs and give them adequate individual attention - 40 dogs, four staff and that is simply impossible - financially.[3-2]

No where is there more concern for the welfare of the dogs than in BAGS racing, otherwise known as 'dog farming', where trainer-owned dogs is now the norm. Owner Richard Newell doubts "the majority of BAGS dogs get a daily gallop out in a field […], more like 10 minutes emptying out twice a day and a trip to the local track once a week running lame for £15."[3-3] It has further been suggested that "trainer-owned dogs form a disproportionate part of those needing but often lacking re-homing. A significant number - so far not reliably quantified - are put down, not always humanely."[3-4]

Viable racing kennels require not only a large number of dogs but also a fast throughput of dogs, not least because a career on regulated tracks will usually not exceed two years (commonly terminating when the animal is about 42 to 48 months young). Some dogs get shifted from kennel to kennel, perhaps ending up abroad or finishing their career on flapping tracks, and of course retirement costs must be kept to a minimum.

Michael Peterson - Oxford Trainer of the Year 2009 and 2010 - was seemingly succeeding where others have failed. Taking over from his father, and with 10 years experience under his belt, Peterson had secured a contract with both Hall Green and

Oxford but he too has found the costs involved on both a personal level and financially outweigh any return. In May 2012 and at just 28 years of age the trainer quit the 'sport', though not necessarily for good… well that was the thinking when the decision to leave was made but subsequent events would dictate otherwise.

In 2009 I caught up with Peterson who, in a series of forthright conversations, gave a candid insight into the hard economics of being a trainer. At the time he had 96 dogs in his kennels and was to remark: "You need that many to pay the bills."

Not surprisingly few trainers will speak openly to anyone outside the industry and so a ruse was needed and provided by way of Chapelane Tom; a greyhound raced and retired under Peterson and subsequently found abandoned in the Croydon area. Luckily the white and black male was soon in a foster home but it would be reasonable for someone involved in his rescue to try and ascertain who the last owner was. This gave me an opportunity to contact Peterson on four occasions across August to September 2009.

It's worth also noting the regulatory body should receive a completed form detailing the fate of all retired greyhounds but no such form for Chapelane Tom was submitted. And though Peterson maintains a record of dogs in his 'care', or so I was told, the relevant book (for greyhounds retired in 2006) could not be found.

Training is a business for Peterson and the retirement of greyhounds is an additional drain on resources: "It's hard to home racing greyhounds; the finances in this sport are piss-poor. A lot of trainers are basically just covering their costs, which to be honest with you I am. I am not making bundles of money, I've got a young family and I have eight to nine dogs here that need homing." Practical, and ultimately financial considerations, have seen an ever increasing number of trainers off-loading greyhounds independently. Peterson worked with a number of rescues but kept his options open: "I'm not being funny, anywhere possible to home a racing greyhound, ye know, anywhere."

The trainer spoke favourably about Greyhounds 4U (G4U); a rescue that interestingly does not agree with yearly vaccinations, conventional wormer or flea treatment.[3-5] Peterson's dogs available for adoption through G4U were on occasion still earning their keep and running. Tragically that was the case for Aintsheapeach. The beautiful blue brindle female had been seeking a home through the rescue since May 2009 but was never to enjoy retirement. On 4 September 2009 Aintsheapeach was put down after breaking her right hock in a BAGS meeting at Oxford. Asked how many dogs he had lost at the track in 2009, Peterson replied: "This year, probably four." That was across a nine month period and not considered high.

Aintsheapeach is one of a staggering 129 dogs to run on regulated tracks under Peterson during 2008. 69 greyhounds ceased running under Peterson during the same year of which 31 are not subsequently recorded racing (under a different trainer). Only six greyhounds from the latter figure were listed on greyhound-data.com either available for adoption or adopted.[3-6]

Above figures highlight a movement of greyhounds that will likely surprise many outside the business of racing. Murtz Keano ran in Ireland before running in Britain under trainers S. A. Cahill, E. Hall and M. Daniels. The greyhound subsequently ran just four races under Peterson at Oxford and finished his career on the track at Odense (Denmark). The dog is now recorded deceased. A flavour of Peterson's operation and the movement of dogs are provided in the tables below.

In October 2009 Peterson was seeking a new race owner for black female Reisk Ruby. Born July 2007, the dog was offered for sale "due to new stock arriving." The terminology he uses is of course highly appropriate for a 'sport' in which the greyhound is just a commodity - essentially a betting medium - that official's record in 'units'. Ruby commanded £800 o.n.o., a relatively modest sum for a dog of her age and recent A3 grading.

The financial difficulties facing trainers are further compounded by the 'elusive' owner, as Peterson explains: "Say an owner gets himself into debt for some reason or can't afford his kennel bill no more, suddenly you can't get hold of the owner and then you've got three or four dogs lumbered with you. And to be honest with you 90 percent of the time that's what happens." It's a problem that has left Peterson significantly out of pocket:

> I've got one owner that has moved up to near Newcastle and I can't get
>
> hold of him. He basically owes me nearly £3,500 which in this sport is a
>
> hell of a lot of money… He's got one dog here, she's four years old, okay,
>
> so she's probably got about three to six months left in her racing career
>
> tops and then basically I am lumbered with the bitch. I am lumbered with
>
> the bitch now because I can't get hold of him.

Peterson's finances were further stretched in 2009 after he was found in breach of rules 174 (i) (b) and 217 at a disciplinary committee hearing on 14 April and fined £600. The judgement was made in relation to a urine sample for greyhound Arco Grace that proved positive for procaine. Grace was later available for adoption through G4U but then placed with Oxford RGT who collected the dog from Peterson's kennels on 6 October 2009. Barry Hebborn, speaking on behalf of the branch, said of the dog: "It's the worst bitch [health wise] we've ever picked up from any stadium and in actual fact he [Peterson] should be reported to the RSPCA."[3-7]

In May 2012 and coinciding with Petersons planned departure the trainer was made a "warned off person" and find £5,000 when further urine samples for greyhounds Buckfast Kid and Babette proved positive for timolol; a beta-blocker likely to impair the animals performance. It was noted at the subsequent disciplinary hearing that the breach in rules was "committed with profit as the motive which might seriously undermine public confidence in greyhound racing."[3-8]

Peterson may feel hard done-by on the outcome of the hearing but was invited and failed to provide a defence. Any other time and that might have been different and he was a trainer highly regarded within racing and seemingly just what the doctor ordered. He delivered a sprinkling of open runners and had the ability to fill race cards across all grades but what he couldn't do was simply make it pay.

Production line of greyhounds:

Greyhounds raced under trainer Michael Peterson in one year (2008)

From left to right: name of greyhound when raced under Peterson, colour, sex, DOB, last recorded race under Peterson (track, date, classification and grade) and the total number of races recorded for the greyhound on retirement. Data compiled February 2012 and excludes trials.

* Ceased running under Peterson in 2008 and not subsequently recorded racing

** Ceased running under Peterson in 2008 and subsequently recorded racing under a different trainer

Name	Colour, sex, DOB	Track	Date & Grade	Races
Acres Four*	bk d, Nov. 2005	Oxford	16.08.2008 A2	17
Active Rover*	bk d, Mar. 2005	Oxford	07.06.2008 A7	57
Aesthetic Amber**	f b, Sep. 2006	Oxford	20.10.2008 A9	26
Aintsheapeach	be bd b, July 2005	Oxford	04.09.2009 A8	92
Annual Music	bk w b, Oct. 2006	Oxford	09.04.2009 S2	20
Apache Joe	bd d, July 2006	Oxford	26.09.2009 A5	41
Arco Grace	bk b, Apr. 2004	Oxford	30.05.2009 A7	114
Arte Et Labore**	bk b, Aug. 2005	Oxford	27.04.2008 A6	61
Auld Pound*	bd b, May 2006	Oxford	01.11.2008 A8	34
Avongate Ant	bk b, Jan. 2007	Oxford	30.01.2009 A5	44
Avongate Rory	bk d, Jan. 2007	Oxford	17.01.2010 A5	69
Ballyneale Anna**	bk b, July 2005	Oxford	14.06.2008 A6	56
Ballyneale Gayle	bk b, July 2005	Oxford	26.04.2009 A5	28
Ballyneale Kate**	bk b, Feb. 2006	Oxford	10.02.2008 A7	25
Ballynoe Express**	bd d, July 2005	Oxford	14.07.2008 A6	42
Ballysimon Rose	bk w b, July 2005	Oxford	19.04.2009 A9	53
Bewitching Blue	be d, May 2004	Oxford	18.01.2009 A8	159
Bee Three Thirty	f b, July 2005	Oxford	02.04.2010 A9	122
Big Wood*	bd b, Aug. 2004	Oxford	03.02.2008 A9	40
Bing Delta**	bk d, Apr. 2006	Oxford	20.11.2008 A3	80
Black Weir*	bk d, July 2004	Oxford	28.12.2008 A5	75
Blue Tac*	be d, Mar. 2005	Oxford	27.03.2008 A5	39
Blunsdon Star	bk d, Oct. 2006	Oxford	03.01.2009 A5	23
Bo Chorno**	bk d, Apr. 2006	Oxford	20.07.2008 A7	70
Boo Weekley*	f w d, Apr. 2007	Oxford	16.12.2008 A8	3
Bourbon Beauty	bk b, Apr. 2005	Oxford	11.12.2009 A8	83
Broadacres Blue	be d, Apr. 2006	Oxford	10.01.2010 A5	57

Bua Nancy	w bk b, Feb. 2006	Oxford	21.02.2010	A6	41
Buds Big Boy	bk w d, Apr. 2006	Oxford	08.08.2009	A4	50
Burbank Cheney*	bk b, Mar. 2006	Oxford	06.04.2008	A4	5
Burbank Posh**	bk w b, Aug. 2006	Oxford	10.08.2008	A8	65
Carnaree Scholes	bk w d, July 2006	Coventry	25.01.2009	OR	31
Castro Apache*	bk d, Mar. 2004	Oxford	18.03.2008	A4	64
Cat Thief**	w bk b, Jan. 2006	Oxford	18.10.2008	A6	58
Cauldron Hex	bd b, July 2005	Oxford	10.07.2009	A8	88
Cauldron Magic	f d, July 2005	Oxford	14.08.2009	A6	69
Cauldron Spells**	bd b, July 2005	Oxford	24.11.2008	A8	63
Clonhaston Best	bk b, June 2006	Oxford	02.08.2009	A4	43
College Ruby	bk d, Apr. 2006	Oxford	25.01.2009	A7	44
Come On Smiley*	bk d, Oct. 2005	Oxford	23.12.2008	A7	51
Connolly Rebel**	bk d, July 2004	Oxford	31.05.2008	A7	83
Corbally Vienna**	bd b, Jan. 2007	Oxford	22.11.2008	A7	27
Corner Hound*	bk d, May 2004	Oxford	06.02.2008	A5	37
Crackator Severn	bk d, June 2004	Oxford	18.06.2009	A4	78
Cragaknock Beta**	w bk b, June 2005	Oxford	16.10.2008	A2	54
Daisyfield Corey	bk d, Jan. 2006	Oxford	11.10.2009	A7	46
Dalcash Rewind	bk b, Oct. 2005	Oxford	05.12.2010	A7	119
Davrics Flash**	bk w b, July 2005	Oxford	05.06.2008	A9	92
Dromlara Michele	be b, July 2006	Oxford	27.09.2009	A5	54
Droopys Cait**	w bk b, May 2006	Oxford	11.08.2008	A7	45
Droopys Jody	w be b, Nov. 2006	Oxford	07.06.2009	S3	36
Effernogue Magic	bk d, Jan. 2007	Oxford	16.01.2009	A9	11
Effernogue Top**	bk w d, June 2005	Oxford	23.08.2008	A3	63
Elm Heartache	bk b, May 2004	Oxford	08.02.2009	A8	70
Emly Final	bk d, Feb. 2007	Oxford	03.05.2009	A3	46
Emly Park	bk w d, Feb. 2007	Oxford	20.03.2011	A6	77
Farloe Nadal*	bk w d, Jan. 2006	Oxford	01.04.2008	A6	27
Fianna Sable**	bk b, Aug. 2006	Oxford	17.11.2008	A5	58
Finchogue Tutzy	w bk b, June 2006	Oxford	05.08.2010	A6	48
Fossil**	w be f d, May 2006	Oxford	06.04.2008	A5	83
Get It	w f d, Nov. 2005	Oxford	30.04.2009	A2	43
Gortkelly Ben**	bd d, May 2005	Oxford	06.11.2008	A9	68
Graigues Dream	bk b, May 2005	Oxford	15.08.2010	A4	101
Graigues Rock*	be b, May 2005	Oxford	01.04.2008	A2	15
Hellroad Slaney	bk w b, Sep. 2005	Oxford	28.06.2009	A4	42

Holly Choice**	bk b, July 2005	Oxford	02.04.2008	A4	33
Home Mate	bd d, Apr. 2005	Oxford	12.06.2009	A7	59
Indigo Jenny	be b, Mar. 2007	Oxford	26.04.2009	A9	39
Indigo Josie	bk b, Mar. 2007	Oxford	04.04.2010	A8	48
Inus Nofear	bk b, Aug. 2005	Oxford	06.02.2010	S3	64
Jet Black Swifty	bk d, Sep. 2006	Oxford	27.06.2010	A2	35
Jethart Classic	bk d, Apr. 2006	Oxford	18.01.2009	A3	51
Jethart Post	bd b, Apr. 2007	Oxford	20.06.2009	A2	24
Joson*	lt f d, Aug. 2005	Oxford	05.03.2008	A9	12
Kasabian Dancer	bk b, Nov. 2006	Oxford	24.07.2009	A8	14
Keianti*	bk d, Oct. 2003	Oxford	12.01.2008	A5	72
Ko Samui**	bk b, Jan. 2006	Oxford	15.12.2008	A5	52
Lisnakill Delia	bk b, June 2006	Oxford	28.06.2009	A5	23
Majesterial One**	bk b, Mar. 2006	Oxford	20.02.2008	A9	58
Major Fancy**	bk b, Jan. 2007	Oxford	02.11.2008	A9	26
Major Hope*	be b, May 2006	Oxford	20.04.2008	A8	13
Major Precious	bk w b, Apr. 2006	Oxford	18.01.2009	A7	50
Malbay Rooney	bd d, Oct. 2005	Oxford	10.07.2009	A3	26
May Morning Blue*	be b, Aug. 2006	Oxford	15.11.2008	A7	8
Mays Fonze	bk b, Feb. 2005	Oxford	25.04.2009	S4	47
Micks Four**	bk d, Sep. 2004	Oxford	30.01.2008	A9	89
Miss Clara Belle	bd b, Nov. 2003	Oxford	05.07.2009	A9	121
Moaning Kanaka*	bk w b, Mar. 2005	Oxford	12.02.2008	S2	41
Moss Hill*	bk d, Sep. 2005	Oxford	08.04.2008	OR	28
Move Over Dada	be bd d, July 2006	Oxford	16.01.2009	A2	98
Murtz Keano**	bk d, Oct. 2004	Oxford	13.10.2008	A6	51
Musical Major**	bd d, Dec. 2004	Oxford	05.04.2008	A7	74
Mustang Mozart	f d, Jan. 2006	Oxford	02.05.2009	A2	23
Ninth Life*	bk w d, Jan. 2005	Oxford	08.04.2008	OR	55
No Joke Kim*	bk b, Mar. 2005	Oxford	06.04.2008	A6	30
Paorachs Flyer*	bk d, Nov. 2004	Oxford	04.08.2008	A9	64
Plum Smuggler**	bd d, Sep. 2005	Oxford	21.02.2008	A8	76
Pudsey Boy**	bd d, July 2006	Oxford	12.10.2008	A4	31
Puntes Package*	bk b, Sep. 2004	Oxford	20.01.2008	A9	38
Pure Power	bd b, Mar. 2004	Oxford	24.07.2009	A6	137
Raging Santa	bd d, Dec. 2005	Oxford	11.06.2009	A8	55
Regazzoni*	bk d, Dec. 2005	Oxford	13.01.2008	A5	13
Reisk Ruby	bk b, July 2007	Oxford	02.10.2009	A4	77

Roberts Boy	bk d, Mar. 2006	Oxford	15.03.2009	A3	48
Roscahill Jenny*	bk b, May 2004	Oxford	14.09.2008	A3	71
Save The Cashier**	bk b, Feb. 2006	Oxford	19.08.2008	A5	23
Scala Honcho*	bk d, Sep. 2006	Hull	08.11.2008	OR	25
Shelbourne Honey**	bd b, July 2006	Oxford	26.02.2008	A8	51
Shelbourne Paris*	bk b, Mar. 2006	Oxford	16.01.2008	A9	8
Smooth General	bd w d, Aug. 2005	Oxford	12.09.2010	A5	98
Sober Rocket*	bk w b, Sep. 2004	Oxford	09.11.2008	A7	73
Soldier Girl	bk b, Aug. 2006	Oxford	11.06.2009	A7	100
Sorchas Lady	bk b, Aug. 2005	Oxford	26.06.2009	A7	39
Stafford Dreams	bd d, June 2005	Oxford	28.01.2010	A7	106
Staneile	bk w d, June 2006	Coventry	25.01.2009	OR	10
Stay For Luck**	bk b, Aug. 2005	Oxford	26.07.2008	S5	67
Stone Park Woods**	bk d, July 2006	Oxford	01.12.2008	A1	83
Stormy Galileo*	bk d, Nov. 2005	Oxford	11.05.2008	A4	28
Stormy Sinatra**	bk d, Nov. 2005	Oxford	08.06.2008	A9	58
Tilly Take Off**	bk b, Nov. 2006	Oxford	06.11.2008	A3	19
Turbo Billy	bk d, Nov. 2005	Oxford	26.03.2009	A2	41
Ullid Turbo**	bk d, Oct. 2005	Coventry	28.12.2008	OR	96
Unique Package	bk w b, Feb. 2006	Oxford	26.12.2009	A5	53
Valarah	bk b, Feb. 2006	Oxford	02.05.2010	A4	37
Warping Time**	f b, May 2005	Oxford	22.01.2008	A8	40
Wilcos Mate*	bk d, May 2004	Coventry	28.12.2008	OR	50
Winnies Flash*	bk b, Nov. 2005	Oxford	21.07.2008	A6	17
Zax Roman**	bk d, Apr. 2006	Oxford	24.06.2008	A8	63
Zax Wren**	bk b, Apr. 2006	Oxford	26.07.2008	S5	39

From pillar to post

The kennel history of just a few of the greyhounds listed above. From left to right: trainer, first and last race dates, track/s and the number of races.

Castro Apache

M. A. Peterson	23.08.2007 - 18.03.2008	Oxford		10
J. M. Ray	02.03.2007 - 26.07.2007	Henlow		16
B. Berwick	03.02.2007 - 17.02.2007	Henlow		3
G. Lynas	16.05.2006 - 14.11.2006	Brough Park		26
K. A. Macari	03.02.2006 - 07.04.2006	Sunderland		9

Connolly Rebel

	22.06.2008 - 08.10.2011	Roskilde	DK	41
		Bjerringbro	DK	
		Odense	DK	
M. A. Peterson	16.04.2008 - 31.05.2008	Oxford		5
T. Atkins	23.02.2008 - 09.04.2008	Oxford		8
R. A. Pendall	30.11.2007 - 18.01.2008	Mildenhall		3
J. W. Counsell	30.03.2007 - 16.11.2007	Mildenhall		15
	28.08.2006 - 08.02.2007	Galway	IE	11
		Longford	IE	

Murtz Keano

	22.04.2009 - 06.10.2010	Odense	DK	21
M. A. Peterson	09.09.2008 - 13.10.2008	Oxford		4
M. Daniels	31.05.2007 - 04.06.2007	Pelaw Grange		2
E. Hall	12.03.2007 - 12.03.2007	Pelaw Grange		1
S. A. Cahill	01.07.2006 - 15.01.2007	Walthamstow		21
		Romford		
	01.04.2006 - 28.04.2006	Waterford	IE	2

Raging Santa

J. Pearson	27.11.2009 - 16.04.2010	Mildenhall		13
N. Colton	30.06.2009 - 13.09.2009	Oxford		7
M. A. Peterson	06.02.2008 - 11.06.2009	Oxford		17
M. H. Massey	09.10.2007 - 30.01.2008	Oxford		17
	30.08.2007 - 30.08.2007	Clonmel	IE	1

Roscahill Jenny

M. A. Peterson	20.04.2008 - 14.09.2008	Oxford		21
T. Atkins	21.02.2008 - 05.04.2008	Oxford		6
R. A. Pendall	02.12.2007 - 01.02.2008	Mildenhall		5
J. W. Counsell	23.07.2007 - 16.11.2007	Mildenhall		12
A. J. Taylor	04.07.2006 - 05.06.2007	Wimbledon		24
		Reading		
	15.09.2005 - 18.05.2006	Galway	IE	3

4

Greyhound breeding scandal

There exists in Britain the Breeding of Dogs Act 1973 that was substantially amended by the Breeding and Sale of Dogs (Welfare) Act 1999. Under the Act a person keeping a breeding establishment for dogs will require a licence issued by the local authority (LA), and for the purposes of the Act such an establishment is defined simply as where a business of breeding dogs for sale is conducted. This definition stands alone and as such would likely encompass the majority of establishments where greyhounds are bred.

That said, a minimum of five litters born in any one-year period would, under the Act, constitute a business of breeding dogs for sale (subject to one or more of the puppies being sold within a given time frame), and it would seem the latter is what is being used as a guideline by local authorities (the Act in my humble opinion is not best worded).

Key detail in the legislation, as you would expect, concerns the welfare and protection of brood bitches, with licence conditions stipulating that any one bitch does not give birth to more than six litters of puppies, and that bitches do not give birth within a 12-month period of last giving birth. All very good you might think but when it comes to greyhounds the Act is seemingly providing little protection.

Track closures and the fall in the number of races held has had a dramatic impact on annual breeding figures - litters recorded with the National Coursing Club (NCC) (covering predominately British litters) falling by more than 65 percent across 10 years from June 2002 - and there are now few establishments that under the 'five litter guideline' would require a licence. Indeed over the last decade the breeding of greyhounds was spread very thinly, with the infamous Charles Pickering ("warned off" in October 2010) being one very notable exception. Other key players include Craig Dawson, James Fenwick and David Firmager, and all three (at the time of writing) were licensed trainers under the GBGB.

The NCC received 55 litter entries (across 24 dams) for Dawson between 1 June 2000 and 31 May 2010 (puppy total: 361). The total number of litters recorded for the above dams was 74 (other litters falling outside the time frame and/or recorded under a different breeder and/or with the Irish Coursing Club (ICC)). And while Dawson has held a breeding licence for many years, there is evidence highlighting the potential repeated violation of license conditions.

Looking solely at litters recorded under Dawson with the NCC, bitches gave birth on 14 occasions within 12 months of last giving birth. When questioned about the above Dawson was to remark: "I didn't know I was only allowed to breed one litter a year per bitch. Nobody has ever told me any different."[4-1] A litter born September 2001 by Plasterscene Gem/Polnoon Lane and recorded under Dawson was the dam's seventh litter, and eight litters are recorded under the trainer for brood bitch Jackies Lady (whelping dates for four of the litters within 12 months of the dam last giving birth).

Breeding data under Fenwick gives even greater cause for concern. The NCC received 101 litter entries (across 45 dams) for the Newcastle trainer between 1 June 2000 and 31 May 2010 (puppy total: 641). A total of 158 litters were recorded for the above dams. The maximum number of litters born in any one calendar year falling within the above dates and recorded solely with the NCC is 18, with five or more litters consistently recorded across any one year period for much of the last decade. Fenwick though was to say that in the last 10 years he had not held a breeding licence.[4-2]

Whelping dates for 40 litter entries recorded under Fenwick with the NCC are within 12 months of the dams last giving birth. A litter born August 2001 by Droopys Zidane/Ladys Guest and recorded under Fenwick was the dam's seventh litter. Brood bitches Lydpal Frankie and Ballybeg Pumpkin are both recorded having seven litters under Fenwick (the latter having a total of eight litters (the eighth recorded under a different breeder with the ICC)), and nine litters are recorded under Fenwick for brood bitch Any Chewing Gum (seven of the litters born within 12 months of the dam last giving birth).

In light of the above it is interesting to note that Fenwick considered the restriction on the number of litters any one brood bitch can have to six as "good and proper." Fenwick, however, not having had a licence cannot presumably be in breach of licence conditions though I would have thought there was a case to answer for operating without a licence.

The Act, perhaps drawn up with the best intentions, is clearly not protecting brood bitches in a number of ways: It depends on the honesty of the breeder (not least in records kept), breeding establishments are seemingly not being monitored as closely as they should be, the legislation is applicable only where the breeding of dogs for *sale* is conducted and the 'five litter guideline' is subject to one or more puppies being sold within a particular time frame. The fact different authorities have different interpretations of the Act should come as no surprise.[4-3]

The only breeder in research carried out where it would appear no puppies were sold within the time frame referenced above is Firmager. His local authority, Melton Borough Council, could not say whether the trainer had held a licence in the past due to records lost in a fire. Firmager was unwilling to talk on the matter, stating only: "We're actually winding down breeding dogs, there's no money in it and to be honest with you I wouldn't have anything good to say about the Greyhound Board of Great Britain."[4-4]

The NCC received 62 litter entries (across 31 dams) for Firmager between 1 June 2000 and 31 May 2010 (puppy total: 457) with five or more litters frequently recorded across any one year period up until October 2009. A total of 74 litters were recorded for the above dams. Whelping dates for 13 litter entries recorded under Firmager with the NCC are within 12 months of the dams last giving birth, and eight litters are recorded under the trainer for brood bitch Fast March (six of the litters born within 12 months of the dam last giving birth).

Comprehensive data compiled in the survey on Dawson and Fenwick was given to the relevant LAs though I question what good it will do. And while the number of breeders that require a licence maybe diminishing, it does not necessarily follow that brood bitches are having fewer litters. Research identified many dams that function simply as 'breeding machines' with litters from any one bitch commonly recorded under different breeders. A period of only seven to eight months in-between whelping dates is not uncommon.

In a submission concerning the Welfare of Racing Greyhounds Regulations 2010, it was the view of the BGRB that "existing legislation relating to the breeding of dogs, and indeed general animal welfare law is sufficient at present."[4-5] Admittedly a predictable comment from the racing industry but it wouldn't be quite so laughable if current legislation was being properly enforced. The GBGB had no wish to discuss the findings detailed above. The Stud Book remarked only that greyhounds do not come in season in line with legislation.

In Ireland (where the majority of dogs running on British tracks (75 to 80 percent) are bred) research has identified brood bitches having up to 10 litters in their lifetime. How effective new breeding legislation for the Republic - the Welfare of Greyhounds Act 2011 - will be remains to be seen… or do we already know the answer to that?

Footnote: Findings detailed above correct at the time compiled (January 2011). Volume 130 of the Greyhound Stud Book (for registrations 1 June 2010 to 31May 2011) includes late entries detailing a further one litter under Dawson and two litters under Firmager that were born within the time frame covered in the survey.

Breeding machines

Breeding history for brood bitch Jackies Lady

Sire	Dogs	Bitches	DOB
Hotshow Ben	2	3	Oct. 2009
Go Wild Teddy	4	3	Mar. 2009
Daves Mentor	1	2	Aug. 2008
Honcho Classic	1	1	Mar. 2007
Droopys Kewell	2	8	Feb. 2006
Top Honcho	5	4	June 2005
Droopys Vieri	4	5	Nov. 2004
Top Honcho	5	4	Feb. 2004

Breeding history for brood bitch Any Chewing Gum

Sire	Dogs	Bitches	DOB
Geordie Parker	1	2	Mar. 2007
Brett Lee	0	1	Feb. 2006
Toms The Best	3	6	Apr. 2005
Kiowa Sweet Trey	3	1	Aug. 2004
Droopys Kewell	1	3	Dec. 2003
Droopys Vieri	5	2	Mar. 2003
Droopys Zidane	2	2	June 2002
Smooth Rumble	5	5	Aug. 2001
Toms The Best	5	5	Oct. 2000

Breeding history for brood bitch Fast March

Sire	Dogs	Bitches	DOB
Droopys Maldini	3	4	Feb. 2009
Droopys Kewell	2	4	June 2008
Top Honcho	4	4	July 2007
Premier County	2	5	Oct. 2006
Droopys Maldini	6	4	Jan. 2006
Brett Lee	1	3	May 2005
Head Honcho	4	6	Nov. 2003
Spiral Nikita	2	3	Jan. 2003

5

Thousands of greyhound puppies unaccounted for

In a conversation with Stephen Franklin - Managing Director, Yarmouth Stadium - the subject of a greyhound recently imported from Ireland came up. The dog was being trialled for the first time and was so nervous it took 50 minutes and the help of all staff to catch the animal. As for his/her fate, "it will go back to the chap in Ireland and that's it," is all Franklin would say.[5-1] I have little doubt the dog would have been destroyed.

The breeding of greyhounds for the purpose of racing is a hit and miss affair at the best of times. Illness aside, both injury and temperament frequently dictate the fate of such dogs. Factor in the inevitable desire for only the highest performing animal, and the 'wastage' figure rises enormously. Even the GBGB concede that a greyhound may never contend a race because the dog "is too slow […], because he or she is disinterested in chasing the artificial hare or because he or she simply interferes or plays with other greyhounds whilst running on the track."[5-2] The industry though will acknowledge little else on the subject and mislead the public greatly on the numbers involved and their fate.

In a House of Commons debate as far back as 1994 a figure of 50 percent was given for the number of Irish bred puppies not making the grade. In the same house and nine years later MP Mark Tami was to highlight his concerns: "About 5,500 [greyhounds] are bred for racing each year across the country. […]. Some 2,000 of the puppies, however, never make it to the tracks; they just disappear. The same problem occurs in Ireland on a much greater scale. We have to assume the worst and accept that they are not all humanely put to sleep by vets."[5-3]

The source and accuracy of such figures is fair to question but they are not dissimilar to more up-to-date information detailed in the May 2007 APGAW report on greyhound welfare. This report included concrete annual numbers for dogs earmarked in Britain and their registration to race under the NGRC, and the data was used to ascertain how many of the greyhounds were never to compete within Britain's regulated sector. Earmarking, however, does not takes place until the dogs are about 12 to 16 weeks old and the assumption was made by APGAW (no doubt for ease of calculation) that all dogs registered to race in any one year were earmarked the previous year (this may or may not be the case). It is further inevitable that a small number of dogs will be registered for racing but progress no further than the trial stage.

Through a rather longwinded process more credible figures can be obtained. Litters are recorded with the NCC, and the number of puppies (for each sex) as found at about four weeks old when a veterinary inspection takes place is given in the Greyhound Stud Book. The DOB, sire and dam is also given and this information can be used to see exactly how many of the puppies will subsequently contend a race on regulated tracks in Britain or, for that matter, are to compete in Ireland or further afield.

The above task I carried out for every litter recorded in Volume 125 which covers litter entries *received* between 1 June 2005 and 31 May 2006 (litter dates will cover a broader time frame to include late entries but excluding a number of litters born leading up to 31 May (and so always balancing out)). The volume chosen provided the most up-to-date information while capturing all dogs contesting a race (Kershope Whisper, for example, not competing until the relatively late age of 35 months).

It was, and remains the largest survey of its kind and had two added bonuses: discrepancies between breeders could be identified and it would for the first time produce a definitive figure for the average greyhound litter size (a contentious issue for many years). Volume 125 catalogued 690 litters. The total number of puppies for the above was 4,338 of which only 2,272 are recorded racing. In other words just 52 percent made the grade.

We have though a black hole in compiling such data. I refer of course to Britain's flapping tracks but this sector of greyhound racing will impact little on the above percentage for a number reasons: the independent sector accounts for no more than about 15 percent of races held nowadays, the vast majority of runners (as within the regulated sector) will be Irish bred, and many competing on flapping tracks do so via the regulated sector. While it may also be possible to find examples where the best bitch in a litter was retired directly for mating (encompassing welfare issues already addressed) it is usual for brood bitches to have competed on the track, if only in a small number of races.

Breeders to stand out in the survey for all the wrong reasons include Charles Pickering not surprisingly, Ann McCarroll (a trainer attached to Brough Park, Newcastle) and Ian Taylor. Litter entries *received* for Pickering (between 1 June 2005 and 31 May 2006) total 39 (not 38 as named in the index), and out of 198 puppies born just 90 reached the naming stage and only 46 (23 percent) are recorded racing (figures in the survey relating to 'naming stage' are based on information in Volume 125, 126 and 127 (up to 31 May 2008)).

All puppies from nine litter entries for Pickering that includes a mating between Goahead Atlantic and El Premier - El Premier being the sire of the brood bitch! - appear to have vanished.[5-4] Pickering lost more than 30 greyhounds to include puppies in a fire at his kennels in December 2006 but the breeder was also the subject of an article in The Sunday Times (11 May 2008) in which he was reported offering slow dogs to be killed for research.

Litter entries for McCarroll total 11, and out of 62 puppies born just 35 were named and 23 (37 percent) are recorded racing. Brood bitches included Agile Milly who, along with other greyhounds, was later rescued after the animals were booked-in at Marske Vets Ltd to be euthanased. And just nine (16 percent) of 55 puppies from 11 litter entries for Taylor are recorded racing. Puppies named total 34 of which 18, curiously, are recorded under Pickering.

For anyone not yet to have done the calculation (4,338 ÷ 690) the average litter size is 6.3. Previous figures floated in the public domain have ranged from 5.2 to 8.0 (the latter used by antis). The variation might seem small until you start looking at the thousands of litters bred annually to meet the demand generated by British tracks. Among industry representatives the commonly accepted figure is 6.4, and so of course they would not dispute 6.3 (it works in their favour).

With this figure we can now accurately determine how many greyhounds are bred in Ireland. Litters recorded with the ICC in 2005 (coinciding with the above survey) total 4,366, and so the number of puppies born is 27,506. It is the British and Irish greyhound racing industries that fuel the breeding of virtually all litters recorded with the NCC and ICC. Britain is big on racing and small on breeding and in Ireland it's the reverse where dogs are frequently raced to sell and the number of races held is below one third the number for Britain.

Based on a ratio of 1:3 we can say that of the total number of puppies born (4,338 + 27,506), about 23,883 were bred to meet the demand generated by greyhound racing in Britain. Deduct the figure for greyhounds registered to compete on regulated tracks (9,751 in 2007) and we are left with a one year total of 14,132 for puppies not making the grade. Even allowing for the black hole that is Britain's flapping tracks and the fact that in Ireland greyhounds are bred also for the blood 'sport' of hare coursing, it is a huge number of puppies to fall by the wayside and of course not all greyhounds registered for racing will progress beyond their trials. I think it would be safe to assume the percentage for Irish-bred dogs to reach competition stage is lower than the 52 percent exposed in the survey carried out for NCC litters. This I would expect where the breeding of greyhounds is generally more a business in its own right.

So what happens to the many thousands of puppies that never contend a race? Interestingly, the GBGB ask the same question under "FAQs" on the group's website (without giving even a suggestion of numbers) but fail to provide an answer, stating only: "Fortunately, young greyhounds can be re-homed very easily."[5-2] I could understand how, to a prospective owner, a puppy would be a more attractive proposition against a veteran of the track that is both physically and mentally scarred (unpalatable as that might be for some people), but in reality how many are being adopted? In a June 2008 report for the Greyhound Forum - comprising representatives from a number of national animal welfare charities and the industry - figures given for *all* greyhounds homed in 2007 are as follows: 4,479 through the RGT and an "estimated" 3,500 by way of owners, trainers and other welfare charities.

How credible the above figures are, is, however, much in question. The Trust's Executive Director at the time, Ivor Stocker, said: "There was certainly instances in the last two or three years were dogs have been counted on more than one occasion because the trainer put in a form and we [RGT] put in a form." Stocker further added that the NGRC "were guilty of counting some dogs not only twice, but sometimes three times or four times."[5-5]

And through the media, the regulatory body invariably compare similar figures solely against the number of greyhounds that retire from racing annually and so, at the very least, imply all greyhounds homed are ex-racers (it looks good and negates the subject of non-graders). The public are being misled. Most, but not all greyhounds homed, are ex-racers. I have brought this subject up twice with the RGT who on both occasions estimated that about 30 percent of the dogs homed through their branches were not registered for racing.[5-6]

If that percentage is applied across all greyhounds homed (I can see no reason why it shouldn't be) and if we assume no greyhounds were counted on more than one occasion (for sake of argument) that is just 2,394 non-graders accounted for in 2007. Homing figures for 2007 are up slightly on 2006, but have risen little subsequently. Indeed in more recent years such figures have fallen significantly. No matter how you look at it, it isn't possible to account for the vast majority of greyhounds not recorded racing.

Eight breeders with litters recorded in the survey showing high 'wastage' were asked about the fate of the puppies. Only one breeder responded, and the response did not address the specific concern of the animals' fortunes. Until the racing industry can provide information to the contrary, one can only assume the vast majority of non-graders are killed, you would hope humanely but sadly that will not always be the case. Indeed as I write this, news is emerging from Ireland of seven or eight greyhounds, in various stages of decomposition and all believed shot, found in a disused quarry. At least two of the dogs were born the previous year (and so no more than 15 months old).

Annual breeding and homing figures have, in the last decade, fluctuated significantly and up-to-date information on the *total* number of greyhounds unaccounted for is covered in "Measuring greyhounds killed."

Making the grade:

Greyhound Stud Book litter entries received between 1 June 2005 and 31 May 2006 and the number of puppies to subsequently be recorded racing

DOB	Litters	Puppies	Recorded racing
May 2006	8	62	37
Apr. 2006	46	300	191
Mar. 2006	28	170	95
Feb. 2006	36	214	107
Jan. 2006	29	148	76
Dec. 2005	34	190	112
Nov. 2005	55	354	175
Oct. 2005	74	487	232
Sep. 2005	70	445	210
Aug. 2005	71	451	242
July 2005	67	447	221
June 2005	77	510	271
May 2005	39	217	133
Apr. 2005	28	190	116
Mar. 2005	16	83	34
Feb. 2005	3	12	7
Jan. 2005	3	19	1
Nov. 2004	1	4	0
Oct. 2004	1	7	1
Sep. 2004	3	20	7
Aug. 2004	1	8	4
Total:	690	4338	2272

Breeders McCarroll and Taylor

Litter entries received 1 June 2005 to 31 May 2006 for Ann McCarroll

Sire	Dam	DOB	Puppies	Named	Racing
Top Honcho	Lamour	Oct. 2005	7	7	5
Top Honcho	Magna Rose	Aug. 2005	6	5	4
Santovita	Speeding Bullet	June 2005	8	5	3
Santovita	Ferndale Monica	May 2005	7	5	3
Hondo Black	Storney Jen	May 2005	4	1	1
Hondo Black	Lamour	Apr. 2005	8	7	3
Droopys Vieri	Hi Fee	Apr. 2005	7	3	3
Droopys Vieri	Below Par	Mar. 2005	5	1	1
Droopys Kewell	Margan Snowbird	Mar. 2005	5	0	0
Droopys Vieri	Agile Milly	Feb. 2005	4	1	0
Droopys Kewell	Stangmore Sue	Feb. 2005	1	0	0
		Total:	62	35	23

Litter entries received 1 June 2005 to 31 May 2006 for Ian Taylor

Sire	Dam	DOB	Puppies	Named	Racing
Knockabout Wok	Coyote Marina	Nov. 2005	5	4 (2)	1
Dutchys Angel	Droopys Sarah	Nov. 2005	8	7 (3)	2
Dutchys Angel	Droopys Justine	Sep. 2005	7	6 (4)	2
Dutchys Angel	Droopys Page	Aug. 2005	7	1	0
Dutchys Angel	Dopeys Fantasy	Aug. 2005	1	0	0
Larkhill River	Survivors Last	July 2005	1	1	0
Dutchys Angel	Quare Duchess	July 2005	3	3 (2)	0
Droopys Corleone	Droopys Corday	July 2005	6	0	0
Dutchys Angel	Coyote Panther	June 2005	4	2 (2)	0
Droopys Corleone	Spenwood Gem	June 2005	5	4	4
Droopys Corleone	Coyote Marina	Mar. 2005	8	6 (5)	0
		Total:	55	34	9

Bracketed figures: puppies registered under Charles Pickering

Findings of the survey correct at the time compiled (February-April 2009). Anomalies on greyhound-data.com with any figures given are due to information recorded incorrectly on the above website (e.g. DOB for Bedrock Tinker (by Top Honcho/Lamour) is June 2006 and not October 2005).

6

The killing tracks of Britain

As the greyhounds hurtle down the back straight in the penultimate race at Hall Green, Birmingham, on 13 January 2010 a stomach-churning crack echoes out across the stadium and Gulleen Star quickly pulls up. According to the dog's trainer, Alan Bodell, the black male had "smashed his hock [left] completely in half." Bodell further ads: "You just have to put them out of their misery as quick as possible... I've been in it [greyhound racing] long enough now to know what happens, it's just not nice."[6-1]

Star was just 41 months young and contending his fifty-sixth race. The average number of races chalked up for greyhounds competing within the regulated sector is about 50, though length of career varies greatly and is frequently brought to an abrupt and sometimes horrific end through injury.

Head Iton Leanne's first race was also her last. The steward's race comment for Leanne's run was "Ck2, FinLm" (checked turn 2 and finished lame). In reality the greyhound bumped 'four' dog, fell and smashed her right shoulder. The beautiful white and black female was carried from the track and later that day humanely destroyed. Her age? 20 months.

In Britain up to six greyhounds are pitted against each other on tracks that essentially comprise two straights leading into tight bends. The forces generated through the limbs on negotiating the turns, the potential to lose footing and inevitable interaction between runners on such tracks, are key factors in the catastrophic number of injuries suffered by the dogs every year. Fractures (commonly hocks, wrists and toes), dislocations, muscle tears and strain, lacerations, puncture wounds, sand burns and paralysis cover broadly the spectrum of injuries, all in the name of entertainment.

Bodell justifies the death of Gulleen Star by saying greyhounds are for racing and the dog was doing what he enjoyed. It's a line repeated by trainers time and time again who further justify the injury toll by referencing horse racing; a 'sport' that in the State of Victoria, Australia, announced a ban on jumps racing at the end of the 2010 season following the death of 'just' 20 horses over a two year period. Pressure from owners, trainers and jockeys overturned the decision but if the death toll was anything similar in greyhound racing, industry officials would be shouting it from the roof tops. As it is, the subject remains one of the most sensitive and guarded within dog racing.

Other greyhounds to break a hock in January 2010 include Glenske Sky, Kilkeedy Blue and Skywalker Brenda. "Statistics indicate that as few as 40 percent of greyhounds with fracture of the hock joint return to the race track" and for the above three it was to signal the end to their lives, but should it have done? [6-2] An account of such an injury is given by champion trainer John McGee in an article examining the work of veterinarian Alessandro Piras:

> I remember one greyhound whose hock just about exploded. It was in a
>
> thousand pieces, I have never seen a worse injury. The owner took the
>
> greyhound to Alessandro to have it put to sleep. Alessandro refused to do
>
> it. He said: 'this greyhound will race again'. [...]. After the operation I
>
> saw the x-ray. It looked as though someone had pulled out a handful of
>
> hair and dropped it on the x-ray plate. There were wires, hundreds of
>
> them, all interweaving. Sure enough the dog raced again. [6-3]

Champion greyhounds maybe afforded the best veterinary treatment - even where the dog is unlikely to race again - because of their value as breeding machines but ten-a-penny graded runners are invariably less fortunate. And of course with a situation where perfectly healthy greyhounds are put to sleep it is inevitable and seemingly commonplace for relatively mild injuries to result in euthanasia. It was to prompt one independent track to post the following message:

> On a number of occasions in recent months the goodwill of the stadium
>
> and vet has been abused by the expectation that any injured dog, however
>
> mildly, will be put to sleep at no expense and on request. [...]. The vet will
>
> continue to euthanase severely injured dogs at his own discretion but will
>
> ask for a £20 donation to be made to a charity of his choice. All other dogs
>
> put to sleep at owners' request (for minor injuries, retirement etc.) will
>
> incur a charge of £30. [6-4]

What the animal cost, age, past and likely future performance, lay-up time and of course the initial outlay for treatment are factors influencing the dog's fate that for Glenske Sky was in the balance. Trainer Gerry Ballentine had the greyhound examined the following day but apparently the injury was a "big job" with "no guarantee there's going to be any results at the end of it." The small detail of which hock it was Ballentine couldn't remember and the black female - a five-year-old veteran of the track with 98 starts - was put to sleep on 12 January 2010.[6-5]

Ardera Express could boast 114 starts but succumb to the hazards of racing while running at Kinsley on 10 January 2010. The black male was bumped and fell on turn one, breaking his neck and killing the dog instantly.

Malbay Katie survived the first corner but sadly not the second when running at Doncaster on 22 January 2010. The blue female was brought down and, in the words of trainer Keith Davis, her right hind leg was "ripped-off" from above the hock. "Every dog went into the corner together and she was the meat in the sandwich," said Davis, who further described the incident as both "horrendous" and "freak." Katie was put to sleep out of sight of spectators watching from the restaurant and bars. Davis sounded genuinely upset when talking about the loss but was philosophical also: "Once the dogs leave the traps unfortunately they are on their own and you have to take what comes."[6-6]

Through speaking to numerous trainers it has been possible to gain a unique insight into the horror of greyhound racing. True, some are unbelievably ignorant, threatening even, but get them on side and information is usually forthcoming. It will likely not have escaped the reader's attention that most incidents detailed above are from January 2010 when I was to enquire about the welfare of 35 dogs. Of those, *apparently* 11 were okay, though two never raced again to include Emerson Brock who lost his life in tragic circumstances.[6-7] The other 24 dogs had suffered injuries varying hugely in severity with eight *known* to have lost their lives.

Fida Cascada and Loughmore Boy were among the more serious casualties. Both sustained foreleg breaks, the former while running at Perry Barr, Birmingham, on 24 January and the latter at Peterborough on 2 January. Both were put to sleep. A coming together with Kangaroo Brice on the back straight put Loughmore Boy into fencing and shattered the leg. "The dog was in such distress… it looked like he was dying of shock," said trainer Bryn Ford.[6-8]

In September 2010 we had what the newly formed Greyhound Owners, Breeders and Trainers Association (GOBATA) described as an "injury crisis." Group chairman Martin White waded in saying: "The matter is of serious concern to practitioners, many of whom have been in touch with GOBATA reporting their individual experiences and frustration at what appears to be an inordinate amount of greyhounds suffering serious injuries."[6-9]

That 2010 was a bad year for injuries there is no doubt - four greyhounds lost their lives as a result of incidents involving "in-running collisions" on the Swindon track in July alone and three greyhounds incurred fatal injuries across nine days in August at Belle Vue - but was the injury toll in either frequency or nature significantly worse than might normally be expected?[6-10] I have no reason to think so.

A race meeting at Belle Vue back in 2004, dubbed "carnage night" by members of the racing fraternity, apparently saw handlers literally queuing up to get their dogs treated. Fast forward to 2008 and a posting by a member of the Belle Vue Owners Forum (BVOF) gives even greater cause for concern: "However the injuries occur, it has been this year [...] the most devastating accumulation of disasters that far exceed recent years. We have also had a catalogue of more minor to serious non career-ending other injuries. Whatever/however these injuries are happening [it] will quite soon wipe out some kennels."[6-11] Across just a four-week period at the same track in 2009 at least six greyhounds were killed as a result of injury.[6-12] I could go on.

And there are occasions when the dogs are pushed beyond what they can physically withstand and collapse and die immediately following a race or trial. For Alis Diamond it was after her sixth race and first win. Two greyhounds - Drumscraw Janet and Cabra Chelsea - both suddenly died within 15 minutes of each other after trials at Hall Green. Irish bred Chelsea was still a puppy and yet to contend a race.

Lives cut short will usually generate a response along the lines 'condolences to all connections' but there is little room for being sentimental in greyhound racing. Injuries and fatalities come with the territory and I have in my work wanted to gain a better understanding on scale, both past and present. To this end a thesis by Brian Agnew was of particular interest, likewise the findings of a recent study of racing comments and results for all meetings staged on regulated tracks in 2010. The latter also generating an unexpected response in the Greyhound Star.

Injuries, Perry Barr

In a thesis presented for the Diploma of Fellowship of the Royal College of Veterinary Surgeons, Brian Agnew examined a record of injuries across 953 race meetings from 1976 to 1984 at Perry Barr. The venue was converted from a grass/sand track to a modern all sand facility in 1978 and data was examined from both before and after the change in the running surface was made. Data relating to the modern facility - not unlike the tracks we have today - covered 748 meetings for which 1,612 injuries were recorded. This was broken down as follows:

		Left	Right			Left	Right
Shoulder	205	64	141	Hindmuscle	227	63	164
Carpus	475	111	364	Hock	58	2	56
Metacarpus	24	8	16	Metatarsus	5	3	2
Forefoot	127	62	65	Hindfoot	144	53	91

Further statistics classified under 'cramp', 'combination' and 'miscellaneous' totalled 234, 54 and 59 respectively. Of the 58 hock injuries listed above, records show that two of the greyhounds were retired and 21 were destroyed. This data, however, is based solely on the immediate post-race decision. The fate of any of the greyhounds on leaving the track is not known.

Notable are comparisons in data collated for the different running surfaces. Injury rates, as a percentage of runners, rose from 4.6 for the year prior to conversion to the all sand facility to 6.6 for the year following conversion. The percentage rate for the all sand facility does later fall (3.9 being the lowest figure) but figures do not show a significant improvement in terms of overall safety. Single limb injuries, as a percentage of total injuries recorded, rose from 65.2 for the grass/sand track to 81.2

following conversion. Sand only tracks, however, reduce the number of races/meetings lost through bad weather and permit a greater frequency of meetings.

The survey at Perry Barr is one of a number of similar studies both in Britain and abroad across which, it has to be said, there exists a lack of uniformity in the recording of information and findings. Where consistency does exist is in the analysis of data and evident correlation between numerous injuries and track configuration. Agnew concluded that the principal causal factor for injury patterns was the "definite and set task demanded of these athletes; the racing at speed on tight, anti-clockwise tracks."[6-13]

A steward's eye view

On British tracks every week the safety of literally thousands of greyhounds is put at risk. To give a full account on the nature and incidence of injuries incurred or a figure for greyhounds euthanased as a result of injury is not possible, but what we do have are the stewards racing comments covering the performance of each dog in each race. How the dogs perform is of course a measure of safety and the commentary, albeit very scant, makes for sobering reading.

In 2010 the number of runners not finishing (DNF) or finishing at distance (DIS) was 4,513. The tally of runners recorded broke-down or lame was 1,812. Above figures cover the races held on tracks governed by the GBGB and formed part of the largest survey of its kind. True, a greyhound recorded DNF or DIS is not *always* an indication of injury, but it is of course the more severe injuries prevalent in greyhound racing that either impair greatly a dog's time or terminate his/her race.

The highest figures recorded for individual tracks are: 68 DNF (Monmore), 290 DIS (Crayford), 231 broke-down/lame (timed finish) (Sittingbourne) and 296 broke-down/lame (overall) (Sittingbourne). The track with the highest listing in the survey was Crayford: 417 runners. Sittingbourne had by far the highest overall figure as a percentage of races staged: 20.9. On 15 January alone stewards at the Kent track recorded one greyhound broke-down and 11 greyhounds lame. A further two finished at distance after falling. For seven of the greyhounds it was to be their last race.

The most serious injuries suffered by the dogs, to include long-bone fractures, are commonly the result of a fall, and the number of runners brought down on oval tracks is nothing short of horrifying. From the data compiled above that covers 5,565 runners, 2,315 are *recorded* falling. The breakdown is as follows: turn one 1,309, turn two 283, turn three 272, turn four 81 and others 370.

Figures clearly indentify the first corner as the most dangerous point on the track and the incidents that occur as the dogs hurtle into turn one account for many of the greyhounds lost through injury. 1,938 runners listed in the survey did not contend another race of which only 188 are listed on greyhound-data.com as either available for adoption or adopted (correct at the time compiled: July-August 2011).[6-14]

Many readers might find the results of the survey disturbing but it does nothing more than provide a flavour of what is happening on British greyhound tracks. It did not include figures for dogs recorded 'cramped', 'faded' or 'stopped'. Nor did it cover the

11 (at the time) independent tracks where it is thought safety is no better, or the tens of thousands of trials held annually.

Furthermore, there is stark variation on what stewards include in race comments that at best highlight only a fraction of the injuries racing dogs incur.[6-15] Seven greyhounds were apparently injured in the course of just one BAGS meeting at Belle Vue in March 2010, according to a BVOF posting, but only three are picked up in the survey (to include Afflecks Palace who was put to sleep).[6-16] And there would seem, with some stewards and one track in particular, a conscious decision to never directly highlight (mark a dog lame or broke-down) an injury sustained. Of course a dog not finishing or finishing at distance cannot be hidden.

GBGB 'retirement' forms include a section for dog's euthanased due to injury (treatable or otherwise) and a request was made twice (12 and 19 September 2011) for the figure covering 2010. The governing body, not surprisingly, never responded. A summary of the survey results posted online did, however, get a response from Greyhound Star editor Floyd Amphlett:

> I was recently forwarded a link to an anti website which claims to have carried out a major survey into racing injuries. [...]. My problem is I can never quite make up my mind with antis. Are they being deliberately devious or do they really believe this stuff? Besides, it isn't all misinformation, and there are some facts quoted that make uncomfortable reading. There is a proven reference (I double-checked it) to one particular meeting - at a BAGS track though not a BAGS meeting - where 12 greyhounds are officially recorded as having finished lame by the stadium vet. Of those at least five suffered career-ending injuries - all at one meeting! It is perhaps no surprise that this particular track found itself subject to a 'hush hush' internal industry review which, in turn, led to a beefing-up of GBGB powers to suspend an unsafe track (until now I was aware of the investigation but hadn't been able to identify the particular race meeting). In conclusion, this type of incident should never be allowed to occur again, not because the antis find it unacceptable, but because we do![6-17]

As the author of the survey I can tell Amphlett that yes I do "believe this stuff" and all figures compiled can be verified. What I had no knowledge about was the 'hush hush' review and I thank Amphlett for its mention (though he 'forgot' to name the track (Sittingbourne)). Finally, if the GBGB used their powers to suspend all unsafe tracks there would be no greyhound racing in Britain (under the Rules of Racing, that is).

Track results survey: Sittingbourne 2010 (excluding trials)

	Race total	DNF	DIS	B'down/lame (timed finish)	B'down/lame (overall)
Jan.	111	3	8	23	28
Feb.	135	3	9	10	15
Mar.	151	3	8	27	32
Apr.	178	3	13	31	37
May	153	5	8	13	19
June	144	2	8	26	30
July	179	6	9	31	40
Aug.	167	6	7	19	27
Sep.	128	2	6	9	12
Oct.	160	5	10	19	26
Nov.	154	5	7	16	20
Dec.	127	1	6	7	10
Total:	1787	44	99	231	296

Track results survey: Sittingbourne 15 January 2010

From left to right: time, race classification and grade, greyhound, commentary, track time and position.

19.53	A6	Hedsor Georgi	Lame	31.36	4
19.53	A6	Cushie Scott	Lame	31.44	5
19.53	A6	Pennypot Rose	Lame	31.63	6
20.08	A8	Spencers Lane	Lame	31.50	4
20.08	A8	Cabinteely	Lame	32.21	5
20.08	A8	Dunbolg Ace	Broke-down 2	0.00	DNF
20.23	S4	Toosey Bird	Lame	42.76	5
20.23	S4	Dons Bride	Fell 5	0.00	DIS
20.53	A7	Dilemmas Angel	Lame	31.48	6
21.08	A2	Toosey Sonic	Lame	30.85	6
21.38	A4	Hedsor Chick	Finished lame	30.87	5
21.38	A4	Verdun Noir	Finished lame	0.00	DNF
21.53	H1	Tommys Gem	Fell 3 badly	0.00	DIS
22.08	A1	Hollyoak Olybean	Lame	0.00	DIS

Just a few of the hundreds of greyhounds to lose their life as a result of injury on British tracks every year

Rooneys Lad, bk d, June 2010 - Feb. 2012 / Knockdrinna West, bk d, May 2008 - Aug. 2011 / Rotar Wing, bk d, Sep. 2007 - July 2011 / Droopys Yankee, dk bd d, July 2009 - Apr. 2011 / Illpayyoulater, bk d, Sep. 2007 - Apr. 2011 / Finlays Meadows, bd d, Oct. 2007 - Apr. 2011 / Cheeky Court, bk b, July 2008 - Feb. 2011 / Melted Fall, bk d, Oct. 2006 - Jan. 2011 / Chase Me Chloe, bk w b, July 2008 - Oct. 2010 / Macbally Linsay, bk b, Mar. 2008 - Sep. 2010 / Isle of Tara, bk b, Mar. 2006 - Sep. 2010 / Ballyverry Rock, bk d, May 2008 - Aug. 2010 / Tyrur Leonard, f d, May 2007 - Aug. 2010 / Sliding Bog, f b, Sep. 2007 - Aug. 2010 / Clubbing Night, bk w d, Sep. 2006 - Aug. 2010 / Daytwo, f d, Oct. 2004 - July 2010 / Wots Er Name, be w b, Mar. 2008 - July 2010 / Lakewood Lass, bk w b, Oct. 2008 - July 2010 / Swift Abel, bk d, Sep. 2007 - July 2010 / Rackethall Kenny, w bk d, Jan. 2008 - July 2010 / Townbrow Sioux, w be b, Dec. 2006 - July 2010 / Highview Pilot, f d, Feb. 2008 - June 2010 / Brizzle Bling, bk b, Mar. 2008 - June 2010 / Ballybride Rover, bk w d, Aug. 2007 - June 2010 / Nervous Basil, bk d, June 2008 - May 2010 / Astrikersfantasy, be b, Jan. 2007 - Apr. 2010 / Killough Boss, w bk d, Oct. 2007 - Mar. 2010 / Afflecks Palace, w bk d, May 2008 - Mar. 2010 / Rebeccas Hustler, w bd b, Apr. 2007 - Jan. 2010 / Fida Cascada, w bk d, Mar. 2006 - Jan. 2010 / Malbay Katie, be b, June 2003 - Jan. 2010 / Skywalker Brenda, bk b, Jan. 2008 - Jan. 2010 / Gulleen Star, bk d, Aug. 2006 - Jan. 2010 / Glenske Sky, bk b, Nov. 2004 - Jan. 2010 / Ardera Express, bk d, Apr. 2005 - Jan. 2010 / Kilkeedy Blue, be d, Jan. 2007 - Jan. 2010 / Loughmore Boy, bk d, Dec. 2006 - Jan. 2010 / Time Cracker, bk b, July 2006 - Nov. 2009 / Oklahoma Trail, bd b, Feb. 2005 - Oct. 2009 / Barra Snowstorm, w bk d, Mar. 2007 - Oct. 2009 / Rookies Fantasy, bk d, May 2007 - Sep. 2009 / Obligation, bk d, Jan. 2007 - Sep. 2009 / Aintsheapeach, be bd b, July 2005 - Sep. 2009 / Mistress Quickly, bk b, Dec. 2006 - July 2009 / Mi Starr, bk d, Oct. 2005 - June 2009 / Fortune John, bk w d, Jan. 2006 - June 2009 / Balreask Touch, be d, Aug. 2005 - June 2009 / Dawn Sunset, bk b, Sep. 2005 - June 2009 / Liam Maldini, bk d, July 2006 - May 2009 / Whinge Bag, be b, Jan. 2007 - May 2009 / Blue Fern, be d, Dec. 2005 - May 2009 / Happy Hawk, bk d, Apr. 2006 - May 2009 / Benlass Panther, bk d, Jan. 2007 - May 2009 / Princess Rocket, bk w b, May 2007 - May 2009 / Westway Pride, f d, Oct. 2006 - May 2009 / Ballymac Mondo, be d, May 2006 - Apr. 2009 / Upalongway, bk b, May 2006 - Apr. 2009 / Coran Singer, be b, June 2005 - Apr. 2009 / Maglass Legend, bk w d, Aug. 2004 - Apr. 2009 / Dainty Express, f d, Oct. 2006 - Mar. 2009 / On The Level, w bd d, Oct. 2006 - Jan. 2009 / Swift Aqua, be w b, Dec. 2005 - Jan. 2009 / Rathtooterny Zip, bk b, Oct. 2005 - Dec. 2008 / Kelsco Girl, bk b, Mar. 2005 - Nov. 2008 / Anduin, be d, Oct. 2006 - Nov. 2008 / Emerson Catkin, bk b, Sep. 2005 - Nov. 2008 / Daves Dasher, dk bd d, Aug. 2006 - Oct. 2008 / Townbrow Mentor, bd d, Dec. 2006 - Oct. 2008 / Bluestone Lane, be d, Apr. 2006 - Oct. 2008 / Hanoi Son, bk d, May 2004 - Oct. 2008 / Glandore Queen, f w b, Sep. 2004 - Oct. 2008 / Frisby Foreman, f d, Oct. 2006 - Oct. 2008 / Corrig Cinders, w be b, Dec. 2005 - Sep. 2008 / Killeacle Rose, be w b, July 2005 – Aug. 2008 / Pigalle Rainbow, bk b, Dec. 2004 - Aug. 2008 / Daltons Lass, bk b, Aug. 2005 - Aug. 2008 / Glaseen Vieri, bk d, Aug. 2005 - Aug. 2008 / Hes A Cheetah, w bd d, Oct. 2003 - July 2008 / Work Of Art, w f d, Feb. 2006 - July 2008 / Mail Madness, w bk d, Dec. 2004 - July 2008 / Will He Rumble, f d, Oct. 2006 - May 2008 / Hillend Lad, be w d, Sep. 2005 - Apr. 2008 / Sarahs Storm, bd w d, Jan. 2006 - Mar. 2008 / Anns Wood, bk b, Nov. 2004 - Feb. 2008 / Carbarns Lenny, w bk d, Sep. 2005 - Feb. 2008 / Head Iton Leanne, w bk b, June 2006 - Feb. 2008 / Dunmahon Boss, bd d, Jan. 2004 - Feb. 2008 / Saleen Rob, bk d, Jan. 2004 - Feb. 2008 / Hi Polejointer, bk d, Nov. 2004 - Feb. 2008 / Barfunkel Craic, bk b, Apr. 2005 - Feb. 2008 / Run On Jess, bk w b, Mar. 2003 - Jan. 2008 / Icecream Charlie, f d, Feb. 2006 - Jan. 2008 / Woody The Tiger, bk d, Dec. 2003 - Jan. 2008 / Marathon Girl, bk w b, Aug. 2005 - Jan. 2008 / Disney Trip, bk d, Sep. 2005 - Dec. 2007 / Calm Aero, bk w b, July 2003 - Dec. 2007 / Lou Be Sure, bk w b, June 2004 - Dec. 2007 / South West Flyer, be d, Jan. 2006 - Dec. 2007 / Killeacle Abina, be b, July 2005 - Dec. 2007 / Greenwell Flash, bk d, Jan. 2004 - Oct. 2007 / Driving Up Hasty, bk d, Apr. 2005 - Sep. 2007 / Tolcas Refrain, w bk b, June 2004 - July 2007 / Our Vieri, be d, Aug. 2004 - July 2007 / Dunmurry Queen, bk b, May 2002 - July 2007 / Bozman Ruling, bk d, Dec. 2002 - Nov. 2006 / Banahoe Panther, bk d, Oct. 2002 - July 2006 / Two One Zero, bk d, July 2004 - May 2006

7

Why Britain's greyhound tracks are inherently lethal

We can now assume that the risk of injury to greyhounds when competing on the track is high… or can we? Actually no, or should I say the act of racing one greyhound against another is not *necessarily* hazardous for the dogs. Take a look at the meetings staged at Odense (Denmark) up until its closure in October 2011 (videos for most of the races can be accessed on greyhound-data.com) and rarely will you see an incident resulting in serious injury. Very significantly, however, Odense is one of only a few tracks where greyhounds run on a straight course, and if properly maintained and managed there is virtually no risk to the dogs.

Britain, sadly, adopted the inherently lethal but commercially attractive oval-like configuration for tracks, made possible with Owen Patrick Smith's design for a mechanical lure. While common to all 35 venues currently in operation (10 independent and 25 regulated), variations exist from track to track in length of straights, banking and tightness of bends. There exists also a huge disparity in the depth of sand (used for the surface and middle layers) and composition of base layer that in turn can affect the performance of the track.

Such variations impact on safety as does the maintenance of the track, operation of lure, trap draw, grade, race distance and weather conditions. Research to date, however, would indicate that even where all factors relating to safety are judged ideal the frequency of injuries will never fall dramatically while dogs are competing on a course that is oval-like in configuration.

Track 'improvements'

In May 2008 the track at Owlerton, Sheffield, received both a new surface and drainage system costing in the region £125,000. General Manager Dave Perry was reported saying: "It is all about the welfare of our greyhounds here at Owlerton. The resurfacing of the track will improve our already high standards."[7-1] Indeed Perry apparently considered the track "one of the safest in the country" prior to work carried out and with no change in its configuration was there ever likely to be a sizeable reduction in dogs injured?[7-2]

A forum posting made in July 2008 would suggest not: "What's going on at Sheffield, injury rates [have] nearly trebled since the track re-laid the surface at massive cost. All sorts of injuries being reported by all trainers: shoulders, wrists, gracilis, hocks [...], there'll be no sound dogs left at this rate!"[7-3]

Similarly, two months following 'improvements' at Yarmouth in June 2010, to include a new surface and drainage, and costing £190,000, owners were reporting a notable increase in the frequency of injuries - many serious - in both trials and races. Though in no way scientific, June at the track showed the highest monthly figure in 2010 for greyhounds recorded DNF/DIS/broke-down as a percentage of races staged: 14.7 (work on the track took place 6-11). The month showing the second highest figure is July: 13.6.

A new surface, however, requires time to bed in (while economic pressures dictate racing will resume immediately) and regardless of any changes made anomalies in injury rates are inevitable. Looking long term I would not expect such rates at either Sheffield or Yarmouth to be higher. By the same token I would be amazed if either were to fall significantly. If we perform the same percentage calculations, again for Yarmouth but this time covering January to May and August to December 2010, the figures are 7.7 and 8.7 respectively.

Yarmouth Racing Manager Bill Johnson, speaking in August 2010, believed the level of injuries had changed little since the work carried out. Perry said the injury rate at Owlerton had fallen but refused to say by how much as he felt the information could be used by those who oppose racing!

Of course it's good PR to claim six-figure sums are being spent in the name of welfare, and I have no doubt that welfare is a factor (injuries to greyhounds are costly for both the owners and the business of racing) but if changes to the track have at best only a marginal impact on safety what other motive could there be for the money invested? A clue can be found on a further posting concerning the work at Sheffield: "Hopefully [it will] make the conditions fairer and remove the bias when the rain comes."[7-4]

Both the promoters and GBGB are seeking to protect and strengthen the integrity of greyhound racing. A good track surface, properly maintained, is a prerequisite for a consistent racing environment. This in turn gives the betting public the assurance that race outcomes are based solely on the dog's ability. Investment, however, is equally driven by a desire, or should I say need, to reduce the number of races/meetings lost through adverse weather; a factor touched on in a discussion questioning the money spent at Yarmouth: "I believe that you are as much aware why Yarmouth management finally had the track drainage done as I am [...], the main reasons given by Simon [Franklin] were the lost meetings last winter [...], as well as the rails' bias that had developed every time the track was salted."[7-5]

Oxford lost four meetings with a further two cut short in February 2012 alone, due to winter conditions. Besides the obvious cost to promoters the cancellation of racing can impact also on kennel strength, pushing dogs 'out of time' and thus having to retrial. It was reported that drainage experts are to "look at the home straight side of the track after a mix of snow and heavy salting caused very boggy conditions."[7-6] And in June 2012 Brough Park, Newcastle, underwent a full re-lay of its track that was to cost a reported £250,000; work that again will address the issue of drainage. Will it result in fewer dogs injured? I wouldn't bet on it though "investment on this scale" will, said Operation's Manager Ian Walton, be "good for the future of greyhound racing."[7-7]

Cornering

Sprinting into a bend increases effective body weight and a human will respond to this by extending the duration of contact each foot has with the ground. As a result, forces on the legs are said to remain constant. A study, however, by James Usherwood and Alan Wilson was to show that, "on entering a tight bend, greyhounds do not change their foot-contact timings and so [in trials observed] have to withstand a 65 percent increase in limb forces."[7-8]

The use of banking will reduce *horizontal* loads and this in turn may see a reduction in the rate of injury. Calculations have though shown the degree of banking required to negate such forces would be so high as to generate additional hazards for the greyhounds as well as proving almost if not impossible to maintain. Further, modern thinking with regard turn one is to keep banking to a minimum, so allowing the outside dogs to remain wide, with the optimum level more a judgement than a science and not easy to ascertain. Attempts to get it right at Oxford in 2009 were described by one member of the racing fraternity as a "fiasco."

At best the bends on a track can be made safer but never safe and injuries are sadly inevitable with the site of injury frequently dictated by the direction of turn. "The most common severe injury, often leading to the dog being euthanatized, is fracture of the right tarsus," notes Ann Hercock, in a thesis part-funded by the GBGB, adding "this injury nearly always involves fracture of the central tarsal bone and of one or more of the adjacent tarsal bones."[7-9] Acclaimed veterinarian Alessandro Piras gives a figure of 96 percent for the incidence of central tarsal bone fractures occurring in the right leg.

The phenomenon was the subject for a thesis by Mary Bergh, who observed: "These fractures have been classified into five types; all of which usually contain a dorsal slab component. The cause [...] has not been rigorously investigated, but it is suspected that racing in a counter-clockwise direction on oval tracks produces cyclic overload of the medial compartment of the right tarsus."[7-10] Jon Dee and Larry Dee further link track configuration with injury patterns:

The fact that the race is run on a circular track, in a counter-clockwise direction, exacerbates the stresses of racing. These increased stresses are substantiated by the locations of metacarpal-metatarsal injuries: they occur most frequently on the 'rail' side of the affected foot, specifically metacarpal V of the left foot, metacarpal II of the right foot and metatarsal III of the right foot.[7-11]

Various studies indentify asymmetrical loading on the distal limbs bones with excessive cyclic loading, ultimately, in many cases, leading to fatigue fractures. Further, decades of breeding that has seen an increase in weight and speed while track configuration remains the same, serves only to heighten the risk of injury. There is no one more vocal on the subject than renowned veterinarian and racing enthusiast Paddy Sweeney:

When I first went to the dogs as a student there was 'little champions' sound to run for three or four seasons. Now there are dogs running at almost twice that weight and about 25 lengths faster. But how long do they last? They may be crippled before they have had 10 races. There is no excuse for being ignorant about the carnage. I have done my duty as a vet to advise people about limiting it (for forty years). The tragedy is that promoters, bookmakers and the sham body set up to protect their interests, seem more interested in exploiting the trainers and the greyhounds for the maximum financial return than in listening.[7-12]

The GBGB apparently consider 36 metres thereabouts "an ideal radius for the bends." Denis Beary, however, of the Canine Sports Medicine Clinic, County Kildare, said of a new tack at Limerick with a proposed radius of 40.8 metres: "In combination with the long straights it is a recipe for disaster."[7-13] Sweeney has expressed a need for straight courses to accommodate the largest of greyhounds now being bred, and where dogs are to compete on a conventional track the "straights should be at least 200 yards apart to allow them to turn without having to lean and get hurt."[7-14]

Dog interaction

While many of the injuries greyhounds sustain are linked directly with the forces generated through cornering, many of the more serious to include long-bone fractures are the result of a collision and/or fall, in other words impact fractures. Even a greyhound running solo risks losing footing on negotiating the tight bends of a track - particularly on shifting sand - and the consequences can be horrific. Pitch six greyhounds against each other and there are an alarming number of incidents in which greyhounds are sent crashing out of a race.

As the survey on stewards' racing comments highlight, the most hazardous point on the track is turn one; a staggering 1,309 runners falling at this point in 2010 alone, to include 121 at Romford. And this was merely those greyhounds *recorded* falling in a survey compiling data solely on dogs marked lame/broke-down/DIS/DNF. It further covered only racing held under the Rules of Racing. The actual number of runners failing to safely negotiate turn one is understood to be far higher.

The tables below help illustrate the sometimes chaotic scenes as the greyhounds hurtle into the first bend. Left to right: greyhound, commentary, time, (and for Oxford) distance and position.

Sunderland, 7 May 2011, race one (19.30 OR)

Elwick Regatta	Badly baulked turn 1	0.00
Queen of Rangers	Knocked over turn 1	0.00
Witton Tom	Checked turn 1	0.00
Ballymac Zigic	Knocked over turn 1	0.00
Cabbies Star	Knocked over turn 1	0.00

Mildenhall, 15 January 2010, race one (19.30 A7)

Shyan Boc	Badly crowded and fell turn 1	0.00
Favour	Wide, crowded and fell turn 1	0.00
Seaside Tina	Badly crowded and fell turn 1	0.00
Fowler Man	Badly crowded and fell turn 1	0.00

Oxford, 18 July 2009, race four (20.20 A1)

Steel Diamond	Very badly bumped turn 1	28.22	12 ½	2
Killishin Sixty	Very badly bumped turn 1	28.46	3	3
Pawseys Pride	Brought down turn 1	30.12	20 ¾	4
Easter Dolly	Stumbled and fell turn 1	30.15	NK	5
Boomtown Prince	Brought down turn 1	30.87	9	6

The chaos witnessed in turn one for the above race at Oxford caught the attention of the media as it followed changes to the track that *hopefully* would *help* alleviate such incidents:

> Recent 'improvements' to the Oxford stadium track, instigated originally by the BGRB, have, in the opinions of many, made the situation a whole lot worse. Baiden [Racing Manager], who only last week said he had not noticed that much difference, agreed that the latest incident on Saturday was a bad one. In that incident Easter Dolly stumbled and fell at the first bend, bringing down Pawseys Pride and Boomtown Prince, while Steel Diamond and Killishin Sixty were very badly impeded.[7-15]

As the dogs hurtle into turn one they are reaching a higher speed than at any other point in the race, though are still "relatively bunched up, reducing their natural tendency to lean into the bend to balance speed and centrifugal forces."[7-16] Further compounding the situation can be railers allotted an outside trap (amongst other less than favourable permutations) and, as owner Andrew Johnston is all too aware, pups running with seasoned dogs: "I had a pup run at Newcastle [...], it was bowled over three times out of eight races at the first bend, a totally green pup thrown in with seasoned adult racers, the poor pup got so smashed up the third time it had to be put to sleep."[7-17]

On trap allocation there is much disquiet but racing managers can only work with the dogs available and the chance of having an equal spread of railers, middle and wide seeds is highly unlikely. Allocation of trap five was brought in question for Knockdrinna West in what was to be his last race. The black male was officially recorded "Crd1&2, CkB3, FinLame" (crowded turn 1 and 2, checked badly turn 3 and finished lame). The unofficial appraisal of his race is a little more revealing:

> Westy had never run out of [trap] five in his life, never had a 'wide' in any of his comments and never run wide in his races. He got smashed on the first bend, on the second bend, for me, is where the dog fatally hurt himself, lost his footing and nearly went down and [he] couldn't take the bend on the third and then broke-down. Was in a bit of shock last night [and] devastated this morning. Condolences go to Yorkie and Jeanette.[7-18]

A track vet was recently to highlight a seemingly not unusual race card consisting of five designated middle seeds, 10 wide runners and 51 railers to include "the ultimate absurdity, a race in which all six runners were railers." Perhaps 'ultimate tragedy' would be a more fitting description for the author's experience of one afternoon at 'the office':

> I found myself working overtime when two greyhounds suffered serious injuries within minutes of each other. Both dogs pulled up lame at the same spot on the track, just where they left the first bend. Lightning proverbially does not strike twice. Both dogs were railers who had the misfortune to find themselves starting from trap five, and in swerving across the track to try and secure their preferred inside berth, both had come to grief.[7-19]

What is described reminds me very much of a well-publicised incident concerning Snip Nua (part owned by comedian Dara O'Briain) and a perfect example of how track bends create also a hazard for the greyhounds on the straight. On this occasion 'six' dog was trailing 'four' dog Nua by about half a length when he moved inside and brought Nua down. 'Six' dog had no where to go but run straight over Nua who in the fall suffered what was reported a hock injury; not terminal but the black female was quickly put to sleep. The dogs had yet to attack the bend - turn one - that, as with all four bends (making up one full circuit) influence, to a lesser or greater degree, the conflicting lines the dogs will run on the straights. Collisions are inevitable.

In short, it is impossible to make racing on oval tracks safe. Read through the racing comments for greyhounds that have chalked up a number of starts and a common theme begins to emerge: terms referencing the interaction between runners - crowded, checked, baulked, bumped, forced, struck into, brought down, knocked over - common to turn one but by no means confined to turn one and linked in most if not all cases to the track's oval configuration.

Injuries, scale

So how many injuries occur and how many greyhounds lose their life as a result of injury? It is impossible to give exact annual figures, even for those tracks governed by the GBGB. The RCPA compile and hold a database on track injuries but information is not being made public, *against* a key recommendation within the May 2007 APGAW report on greyhound welfare. Though it has to be said the industry themselves do not have precise figures. Data compiled is based on track veterinary reports and many injuries are diagnosed only the following day (for the same reason data concerning Perry Barr in the thesis by Brian Agnew is not complete). In a BVOF posting it is said:

> At present only those types of injury that show up quickly stand any
> chance of being recorded and even then may not be when a track vet says
> of a probable serious injury (which it was) 'well I won't record it in case I
> am wrong and the dog can compete in the next round'. This means that
> since trainers do not report injuries later, it was never recorded.[7-20]

It is further alleged that certain trainers who at the time of a meeting suspect a dog to be lame are not always having the animal checked by the vet in attendance. And as already mentioned the GBGB hold figures for greyhounds euthanased due to injury (treatable or otherwise), based on information given in the group's 'retirement' form that covers dogs killed at the track or elsewhere, but again these statistics are not being made public. What information is available, however, gives animal welfare charities and the like at least an indication of scale.

Shortly before Walthamstow closed I spoke with its racing office who stated that about 25 greyhounds were put to sleep as a result of injury at the track over a 12-month period. When Marcus Westgate, Yarmouth's Assistant Racing Manager, was pushed on a figure for greyhounds put down per month he replied: "Maybe a couple, something like that."[7-21] So not unlike Walthamstow where the number of races held across one full year represented 4.7 percent of the total for GBGB tracks (figure based on the venue's last full year of racing (2007)). The same percentage calculation for Yarmouth in 2008 (above quote from October 2008) is a disturbing 2.8 percent.

Carol Hercock's thesis includes data concerning 87 greyhounds killed from June 2007 to August 2010 at just one track - not named but thought to be Belle Vue - with 80 having incurred "severe" injuries during racing and three suffering "health problems" resulting from racing.[7-22] So again a similar figure, allowing for the period of time covered. Belle Vue stage more races annually than Yarmouth but less than Walthamstow's last full-year total.

We have in addition those greyhounds injured at the above tracks and subsequently put down away from the stadium. Perhaps such figures account for the majority of fatalities as it has been claimed "many tracks operate a policy whereby very few greyhounds are put to sleep at the track. Trainers are advised to take them home and see their own vet the following day. It is a wonderful policy for distorting figures."[7-23] Of course no vet fit to practice would refuse to end the life of a greyhound seriously injured and suffering but there are many injuries where the greyhound can be made comfortable and assessed later; injuries that terminate the animals racing career and though not life-threatening ultimately result in the animal being destroyed.

In Agnew's study of veterinary records for Perry Barr a ratio of 1:4.3 is given for the number of injuries per race on the all-sand facility. That translates to a figure of 14,000 for injuries recorded by track vets across the regulated sector in 2011, *excluding* trials. And of course any such figure based on Agnew's findings covers, in the main, only those injuries of a more serious nature that are identified immediately post race. Some industry officials might argue that tracks have got safer since the data on Perry Barr was compiled but at the same time greyhounds have got heavier and faster. Try and convince the likes of veterinarian Paddy Sweeney that racing nowadays is safer and you will no doubt fail. Indeed if reports from grass-roots members of the racing fraternity are anything to go by, recent years have been as bad as it gets.

Another indication of scale is the fact that at any one time a professional trainer may have as many as half his/her dogs out through injury. Not surprising when you consider "up to 50 percent of greyhounds develop varying degrees of musculo-skeletal injury or metabolic stress during each hard gallop or race. These injuries can range from minor wear and tear injuries to the muscles and bones, to more severe breakdown injuries."[7-16] The majority of retirements, it has further been said, are down to injury and not old age.

From a wealth of information, to include the feedback gained from speaking with dozens of trainers, it would be reasonable to assume the number dogs to lose their life as a result of injury in either trials or racing runs into many hundreds over any one-year period for the regulated sector alone and may, to put this into context, represent about 10 percent of annual registrations for greyhounds to compete under the Rules of Racing (a little below 8,000 in 2012). Include those greyhounds competing on Britain's flapping tracks and it is possibly a four-figure total.

Using Agnew's ratio for injuries per race we have been able to gain an idea on the number of injuries *recorded* within the regulated sector but what of the actual number, minor through to serious, across both sectors of the industry? One can only hazard a guess but I would not discount a figure running into tens of thousands annually, as opposed to merely thousands. It is easy to see why this subject remains one of the most sensitive and guarded within greyhound racing, and I haven't even touched on those injuries incurred during schooling. If this was horse racing it would have been banned years ago.

Footnote: While many references are made to specific incidents or characteristics of British tracks and racing the theory is relevant to racing on oval-like configured tracks around the world and that is why at any such track a catalogue of injuries occur (see p. 89 for American examples); further evidence if it was ever needed that such tracks can never be made safe.

8

Failing in basic care

In 2011 "Kicking off with Colin Murray" - a seasonal show broadcast on Friday evenings on BBC Radio 5 Live - began following the fortunes of greyhound Showme Thebunny; a white and brindle bitch trained under Norman Melbourne and running at Owlerton, Sheffield. With an audience of 700,000 and a pro-greyhound racing team of presenters willing the dog on each week it was an "opportunity to showcase all the excitement the sport so readily offers up."[8-1] Within two months, however, the marketing coup had backfired.

In reality racing dogs spend a matter of seconds in competition and the majority of time hidden from public view in trainers' kennels where conditions and care so frequently leave much to be desired. A video of Bunny's kennels, that are licensed and inspected by the GBGB, appeared on YouTube and depicted ramshackle buildings, all manner of waste strewn across an isolated site, dog faeces and soiled bedding in a purposely dug pit and similar material, partially burnt, in an open skip. The dog, previously named Rhincrew Snowey, was quickly dropped from Murray's show, moved to different kennels and in January 2012 retired from racing.[8-2]

Shortly following Bunny's retirement the appalling conditions of a further two kennels were being made public. Monitored during October and November 2011, the initial account (below) covers key observations at trainer Nigel Saunders' kennels based in Stockport:

> Many dogs were kept in unheated brick sheds with old corrugated tin sheet
>
> roofs. Small squares cut out from the doors provided the dogs with their
>
> only source of natural light. […]. Two large kennel blocks constructed of
>
> brick and corrugated asbestos/tin sheet had little means of natural light. In
>
> one block there were just a few skylights and although the second block

had two large windows, they were blacked out from the inside. Electric lights were only turned on for cleaning and the kennelling of dogs returning from the track, leaving the dogs in virtual darkness for most of the day. [...]. There was no evidence of heating or mechanical ventilation and the dogs clearly suffered in the urine-soaked atmosphere that investigators said they could smell from a distance of 30 feet from the kennels. On the perimeter of the property dog faeces and soiled bedding had been dumped over what must have been [a period of] many years, resulting in a huge mound of toxic waste; a serious breach of environmental legislation.[8-3]

Saunders supplies dogs for Manchester's Belle Vue track, as does the other trainer, Beverly Heaton, whose kennels were monitored. Based in Swinton, findings at Heaton's kennels are equally disturbing:

Dogs were kept in shoddily built tin shelters or Air Europe cargo containers with no doors, and blue plastic food containers were used as beds. While other shelters were made of brick, they had no doors or visible signs of bedding [...]. The small muddy paddocks were littered with faeces and reeked of urine. Although a kennel block had been freshly painted the walls were stained with penetrating damp and water leaking from the roof. Most dogs had to share a bed barely big enough for one and Dacent Alonso was muzzled even though he was kennelled alone. [...]. Faeces, soiled bedding, commercial and household waste were burnt on a large bonfire, in breach of environmental legislation.[8-3]

In her defence Heaton is reported as saying: "We're inspected by the GBGB once a fortnight and if there was a problem they'd soon tell us."[8-4] Above examples highlight accepted standards on the part of the governing body and stewards carrying out inspections. At the same time the industry recognise the need for improvement and in 2012 were reportedly progressing on a £200,000 project to bring a large number of kennels up to minimum standard. Whether the above, however, is driven by any real concern for the dogs is open to question: "When the Animal Welfare Bill was introduced, many welfare organisations demanded that UKAS checks should extend to licensed kennels, in addition to racecourses. Although that idea was temporarily shelved, the GBGB is aware that there could be renewed calls for that extension when regulations are reviewed in 2015."[8-5]

The conditions of trainers' establishments take on further relevance when you consider racing dogs are generally kennelled for about 23 hours a day. Frequently two dogs will share one small kennel and bed, and muzzles are used as a long term solution where fighting may occur. On the latter point the RSPCA has said:

> Muzzles are sometimes necessary as part of responsible dog ownership, however they should not be used as a long term measure. If such measures are needed this highlights the fundamental problems with the way greyhounds are kept at present. The Society is extremely concerned at the management techniques currently used, such as kennelling in pairs but only allowing the dogs the use of one bed thus increasing the chances of fighting.[8-6]

There is a duty of care under Section 9 of the Animal Welfare Act 2006 that specifically addressing the "needs" of kept animals, to include greyhounds though you would be forgiven for thinking otherwise. For the purposes of the Act those needs include: a) a suitable environment, b) a suitable diet, c) to be able to exhibit normal behaviour patterns, d) any need to be housed with, or apart from, other animals, and e) to be protected from pain, suffering, injury and disease. Section 9 is, in the view of the RSPCA, "likely to pose a significant challenge to many trainers, as many kennels are far from adequate to meet this requirement."[8-7]

It was alleged dogs under Poole trainer Eve Blanchard endured soiled bedding and a lack of fresh water or any form of exercise for three days at a time.[8-8] The allegations, made by kennel hand Neil Haine, came some six months after conditions at the kennels had been exposed in undercover video footage. Taken in May 2008 and prior to Haine's employment, the footage highlighted concerns to include inadequate provisions, a leaking roof and no lighting, with a number of dogs only visible in the footage with the use of a torch.

It prompted intervention from the RSPCA. Inspector Ken Snook ordered a number of structural improvements to be made but compliance of the order was left with the GBGB. Blanchard's kennels, based in Shillingtone, Dorset, came under the jurisdiction of Stipendiary Steward Colin Betteridge who, though aware of problems, felt there was "no serious issue" and "nothing to be alarmed at."[8-9]

You pray for the speedy retirement and adoption for greyhounds living in such conditions but Blanchard's dogs are sadly not so lucky, according Tracey Seymour (then representing Devon and South-West RGT): "She doesn't home her dogs with anyone. She lets them rot and die in her kennel… She's the world's worst nightmare. She's one of those trainers that believe a greyhound should spend the rest of its life in a kennel, rotting until it dies, and then she gets people to go round there and dig holes and bury them." Seymour spoke with the trainer when first linking-up with Poole stadium, in the hope some of the dogs could be found loving homes but said Blanchard "wouldn't budge, she wouldn't give her dogs over to a homing scheme at all."[8-10]

Graham Holland is a trainer but nonetheless has publicly criticised members of his own profession on standards of care: "I don't know how some of the trainers get licences. Britain is obsessed with welfare for the older dogs, and rightly so, but they should look more closely at the welfare of racing dogs."[8-11]

How it is professional trainer Ronald Paterson holds a licence is a question likely asked by a number of people, though it was suspended briefly in 2010. As far back as April 2008 Paterson was in the news when he failed to gain retrospective planning permission for his kennels near Eaglescliffe, Stockton-on-Tees. Matters concerning the welfare of his dogs were raised at the time and this came to the fore two years later in an article documenting a number of allegations to include no overnight supervision for the greyhounds, overcrowding and dogs kept in outside pens in freezing weather.[8-12]

The suspension of his license was for just six weeks when, at a disciplinary committee hearing on 8 June 2010, he was found in breach of rules 152 (i) and 212 (xx) for the lack of supervision, but concern for the welfare of his dogs remained. Over much of the latter half of 2011 Paterson's kennels were privately monitored and findings were e-mailed to the GBGB. It was alleged greyhounds received attention only between the hours of 8.00 and 10.30 in the morning, kennels lacked heating or natural light, the site was imbedded with rubbish and again without overnight superivision.[8-13] Further issues were raised in a second e-mail to include a failure "to keep accurate records for the greyhounds and maintain documentary evidence as to their disposal."[8-14]

Speaking from personal experience it can be frustrating bringing issues of welfare to the attention of the GBGB, as I am sure the author of the above e-mails would testify: "As usually my complaint is ignored in the first instance, then I usually receive a rude response from you."[8-14] The complaints made did later come under the scrutiny of Investigating Officer Clive Carr but Paterson kept hold of his license. Priorities are understood and conditions described above, while affecting the dogs' well-being, will not prevent dogs racing.

Kennels poorly constructed and inadequately fitted out are far from suitable for greyhounds in particular as their short coats and low fat reserves provide little protection against low ambient temperatures. Heat loss can in turn affect metabolism and "make the animal more vulnerable to physical stress and cause reduced immune function and defence against infection."[8-15] Between 18 and 20 degrees Celsius is said the ideal temperature to maintain in racing kennels in winter conditions (and no higher than 23 degrees in summer), though if you put that to trainers expect to be laughed at. Blanchard believed the little heat generated by a group of dogs living within a confined area, and sound proofing installed more than 20 years ago helps keep the dogs warm when temperatures plummet.

Widespread dental and gum disease in racing dogs illustrates perfectly the priorities for trainers. Periodontal disease is well known in greyhounds, so much so it is commonly assumed a genetic problem, but it does in fact relate directly to their diet; a diet suitable only for racing. Of course racing dogs lack the treats and table scraps that many pet dogs enjoy and that do nothing for dental hygiene, but racing dogs lack also much or anything in the way of solids that act as an abrasive force essential in keeping teeth clean and preventing the onslaught of more serious issues. It's a diet often referred to as 'slops' due to its consistency, a diet high in protein but lacking hard biscuits to bite into. Hide chews, beef bones in particular, and brushing will shift plaque but we are now entering the realm of fantasy where racing dogs are concerned.

No organisation is aware of the problem better than the RGT where the cost for dental treatment is reportedly second only to neutering in veterinary expenditure. The charity was presented with a bill for £363 to cover the work carried out on one greyhound; a three-year-old bitch who required all but four teeth removed. RGT co-ordinator Amanda Ainsworth said that in such a young dog "this is down to neglect, pure and simple."[8-16] More recently the charity took in 39 dogs from a site licensed by the GBGB and many had severe dental related problems to the extent four were put to sleep. The appalling neglect witnessed emphasised, in the view of Ainsworth, "the industry's ongoing failure to tackle the issue."[8-17] Were the trainers in question brought to the attention of the RSPCA and prosecuted? I understand not.

It further brings into question the priority of track veterinarians. Greyhounds rescued and found to be in a sorrowful condition have varied histories but include dogs not long since filling race cards. Dollar Baby, trained under Thomas White, was running at Doncaster when trainer Keith Davis and partner Sandra had concern for her welfare: "She looked extremely poor [...]. We watched her deteriorate week after week and made complaints about which nothing was ever done." The fawn bitch was apparently four kilos below her best weight and "thoroughly abused" but nonetheless fit to race.[8-18]

And where veterinary instruction is given will it be heeded? Not in the sad case of Dunmurry Queen. In a messy low grade race at Yarmouth the black bitch sustained a serious injury that was dealt with "efficiently" by the track vet. Issued at the time was a) a letter confirming the medication prescribed and instruction to present the dog to a veterinary practice within two days, and b) a written direction and transport certificate confirming the dog is to be x-rayed. Owner John Poll, however, gave "specific instruction" to her trainer Michael Clare "that no vet was to be involved." A week later the greyhound was retuned to Poll and 12 days later put to sleep following intervention by the RSPCA.[8-19]

The above case was dealt with internally as were the circumstances leading to the death of Pearly Black who had yet to contest a race. Described as a "very nervous bitch," this poor greyhound was discovered in emaciated condition on a steward's inspection of trainer Martin Dowman's kennels. Located in Lincolnshire, the apparent tremor of an earthquake some three weeks earlier was given as at least a contributing factor. The greyhound - just 15 months' young - and trainer was accompanied by the steward to a veterinary practice where it was decided the animal should be put down. Dowman attended a subsequent NGRC inquiry because, in his words, "I thought they were going to crucify me," but with the penalty being merely a severe reprimand and £650 fine the trainer was "quite happy."[8-20]

The GBGB PR machine will have you believe the 'sport' of greyhound racing is "well run, properly regulated and the welfare of the dogs is always the main priority of those involved."[8-21] I'm not sure many volunteers involved in the rescue of greyhounds would agree, and not least Chair of Lancashire and Belle Vue RGT, Sarah Horner. In 2011, and before the branch was affiliated to Belle Vue, Horner publicly spoke out about life on the 'front line' and helping dogs "with maggots crawling out of festering wounds" and "covered in crap and pee, and emaciated." The volunteer further accused owners and trainers of dumping greyhounds on branch doorsteps and threatening to have the animals destroyed if not taken in, adding: "I had one Belle Vue owner bring a dog to me whose back leg was dangling the wrong way round. He had it in his arms and shoved the dog at me and said 'see what you can do with him' [and then] laughed and walked off."[8-22] Not representative? According to Horner the above is an example of what is seen at many non-track based RGT branches.

It is very evident that what is required is not only a major upgrade in kennels but also a change in mindset. At a rescue not identified a trainer the sort of which Horner is seemingly familiar "practically threw the lead at staff with the instruction 'There is no point in trying to re-home this one; he's a nasty bastard, you might as well put him down now'." The dog in question had in fact a "gentle manner" and soon found a home.[8-23] Trainer Anthony Lucas presented a huge challenge for all concerned when, in July 2011, he "deliberately abandoned his kennels without any regard for the welfare of the [70] greyhounds in his charge."[8-24] A kennel hand was left to cope the best she could and Lucas later received the maximum sanction allowed under the Rules of Racing when made a "warned off" person and fined £5,000 (though I would not expect the fine to be paid, in common with others who have incurred the same penalty).

There are of course good trainers as well as bad trainers and good kennels as well as bad kennels but failings in basic care, some 87 years after the first meetings were staged on British soil, remain both endemic and wide-ranging. Ainsworth has estimated (Greyhound Star, June 2011) that a staggering 30 to 40 percent of dogs placed with the RGT (and I have no reason to think the percentage would be less across independent rescues) have fleas and worms. At the other end of the scale there are truly appalling cases putting in jeopardy the lives of greyhounds. And what should be of equal concern is that where cases of neglect and cruelty are identified under *licensed* trainers, it is virtually unheard of for those cases to be dealt with independently and through due process of a magistrates' court, where proportionate justice would be seen to be done.

9

Greyhound homing scandal

In April 2012 the Sunderland Echo covered a story concerning greyhounds Ruby and Alfie, abandoned in Durham and being cared for by Sharon Morgan, a volunteer with Greyhound Rescue Northeast. The condition of the animals had a familiar ring: rotting teeth, emaciated and covered in fleas. Morgan questioned the treatment of ex-racers and is reported saying: "There are some good trainers who will ring us to pick up the dogs, but others just leave them to die or take them to be put down."[9-1] Actually, Morgan missed out a growing category of both owners and trainers who are simply giving the animals to anyone. It makes you wonder about the history of Ruby and Alfie, particularly with the former being 10 years of age.

How to dispose of both non-graders and ex-racers has been an issue for members of the racing fraternity and the industry as a whole ever since the media got wise to unethical and cruel practices rife within greyhound racing. A dog humanely put down away from the track will incur a charge not insignificant for professional kennels wanting rid of many dogs annually, and to this must be added the cost for disposal of the cadavers. Placing dogs with rescues is being encouraged but a 'donation' is normally requested (anything up to £100 depending on the charity, to part cover neutering etc.) and because of limited resources there is invariably a waiting list. The latter point alone will discourage trainers who want 'redundant stock' out, and new blood able to earn their keep, in ASAP.

The solution: direct and indiscriminate homing. Commonly the dogs are advertised 'free to good homes' but don't let that fool you. Some nutter, banned from keeping animals and living on the top floor of a block of flats, could walk away with any number of greyhounds being got rid of in this way. It is a scandal to first catch my attention back in 2007 and I made a point of responding to a random selection of such ads that can usually be found either in shop windows or on the internet (on free-to-post sites: Gumtree and the like). Steve Meazer - one of the trainers contacted - remarked how quickly the animals are gone when advertised. Asked if the greyhound he wanted rid of would be vaccinated or neutered he replied: "No mate, I don't do anything like that."[9-2] None of the greyhounds I enquired about were neutered and nearly all trainers/owners appeared indifferent about who I was and the home being offered. Meazer boasts homing over 100 greyhounds. Their fate isn't known.

A few years back, adverts submitted by Anne Cossey could be seen regularly. She claims to have homed 500 greyhounds thereabouts but was simply acting as go-between for trainers and owners in Norfolk who were being saved the trouble of advertising themselves. I believe at no stage was any responsible vetting procedure carried out and it is left to the likes of founder of Norwich-based AFG, Annie Boddey, to deal with the consequences. AFG have rescued a number of unwanted greyhounds over the years - greyhounds neglected, greyhounds passed from pillar to post, greyhounds abandoned - and when their history is traced it is found, with a few exceptions, the dogs were homed directly by their trainer/owner. Examples include:

- Blue Belle Jo: two years in the 'care' of an "elderly alcoholic," housed in a dilapidated shed and received little attention.

- Glenske Shade: given away with the same indifferent concern for her welfare that was evident in the very poor condition of the dog.

- Hare Running: four owners identified following retirement and before being signed over to AFG.

- Mistakenidentity: left on his own for 12 hours at a time by his new owner who was not in a position to look after any dog properly.

- No Way Jose: allowed to have several litters and homed in a dilapidated caravan. When responsibility for the animals' care was left with a neighbour the help of AFG was sought.

- On the Dot: his new owner adopted also Drominboy Pretty and sought to make money from a mating. Seven puppies later (advertised for £100 each) the sire was quickly got rid of, as was the dam three months after whelping.

- Elsa Something: signed over to AFG when her new owner - a single mother working all hours - found it impossible to take proper care of the dog.

- Rum Gal: picked up as a stray on the streets of Norwich just months after being homed directly.

- Slieve Gallen: passed on quickly by her new owner and over the following eight months suffered appalling treatment at the hands of Claire Colby who was later banned from owning dogs for five years. The dog was emaciated, flea-ridden and suffering numerous pressure sores.

- Tasmanian Diego: given away just two days after her career on the track was terminated due to injury. Trainer Ian Brown was likely elated when prospective owner, Angela Laver, agreed also to adopt Burgoyne Bunny who had retired through injury four days previously. Unable to cope, Laver off-loaded both greyhounds within a couple of weeks of signing the adoption forms. Bunny was later found abandoned in a flat and Diego spent just three months in her next 'forever' home.[9-3]

Rum Gal: safe in the care of Annie Boddey after being picked up as a stray on the streets of Norwich

Tasmanian Diego: one of a large number of dogs off-loaded every year by Yarmouth trainer Ian Brown

I suspect many people respond to the ads on a whim, for others it is an opportunity to adopt when judged unsuitable by responsible rescues. Some dogs might get lucky but their stories are frequently sad, frequently tragic. Two of trainer Armine Appleton's dogs ended up, I was told, in the 'care' of a drug addict later found dead from an overdose. Another one of his dogs - Sophie An M'daddy (homed through Cossey) - was put down at the request of his new owner for nothing more than being unclean when left in the home alone. I mentioned it to Appleton but he seemed to care little.

Dog pounds, charities and individuals picking up the pieces rarely, to their shame, speak out but that could not be said for AFG. The group has been successful getting media coverage, and dogs rescued are documented on the internet. I raised questions with the NGRC and published an article on the subject, and the upshot of it all was a visit to Norfolk on 31 October 2007 by NGRC Investigating Officer Clive Carr.

All greyhounds running on Britain's regulated tracks come under the Rules of Racing, and Rule 18 covers the responsibility of owners and disposal of their greyhounds. Various options are open to the last registered owner including having the animal destroyed but subsection '1.e' applies when homing dogs directly and it states this action is to be carried out "responsibly." When it was put to Luke Taylor - then NGRC Retired Greyhound Co-ordinator - that it is not responsible to give an animal to someone when you know nothing about the person or where they live, he replied: "I'm not disagreeing there."[9-4] Some kennels may transport dogs to their new home but again, if it's a done deal, how is this in anyway acting responsibly?

Carr, however, had a different view. I remember discussing the matter with him and losing my cool but not without good reason. His understanding of the word 'responsibly' would seem to differ from accepted meaning. Perhaps, as a representative of the regulatory body, this should come as no surprise. Officials no doubt appreciate the difficulties facing trainers and it suits the industry to turn a blind eye. A greyhound indiscriminately homed is still a greyhound homed and collectively annual national homing figures receive a significant boost without any funding from the industry. This data can in turn be used to promote greyhound racing. The trainer wins, the industry wins and who cares about the welfare of greyhounds?

It was business as usual and a quick call to Cossey in March 2008 resulted in the offer of a greyhound bitch from trainer Chris Brooks without any searching questions or need for a home check. Brooks will complete and return an NGRC retirement form (or at least should do) and that's another greyhound the industry can record as homed. Self-regulation serves only to protect the business of greyhound racing but according to the then Chief Executive for the regulatory body, Alistair McLean, "the sport can be proud of the progress it has made in dealing with owners' obligations under Rule 18 and the general well-being and welfare of the retiring racing greyhound."[9-5]

Boddey's work has never stopped and I came back to the subject in May 2010 when a staggering 12 greyhounds were being advertised "free to good homes" in a pet shop based in Leiston, Suffolk. It generated a discussion on the internet and comments to include "what will happen to those not taken" and "how come there are 12 available all at the same time!" Equally, one should be asking what will happen to those that *are* taken.

The person off-loading the dogs was trainer Chris Mosdall - a major player at Harlow (and now Wimbledon) - and when interest was expressed in adopting two of them he sounded delighted. You might guess the rest: dogs not neutered and no home check required, not even questions asked about my situation concerning such matters to include work, home and garden, and while the trainer was led to believe I had never previously adopted a greyhound, little advice was given. Mosdall though had the uncanny ability to tell from my voice that the dogs would be well looked after and the opportunity to get rid of one, possibly two greyhounds, quickly at zero cost is of course incidental.

And Mosdall cannot plead ignorance. The trainer recounted how two young bitches he gave away about five months prior to the ad in Leiston were picked up in the Wanstead area in appalling condition. "The people who do that to dogs should have it done to them, that's the way I look at it," said Mosdall.[9-6] My view is trainers and owners should not be homing the animals as there is a clear conflict of interest. Mosdall was reported to the GBGB because that was the right thing to do and not out of any belief that action would be taken against him. I understand the RGT took what dogs were still looking for a home but what of future retirements?

You cannot, of course, make someone care about the well-being of a dog, particularly when viewed as nothing more than a commodity, and so the option of homing retirements directly needs reviewing. In my conversation with Taylor I was invited to submit ideas on amending Rule 18. The full wording of the relevant section (1.e) states only "the greyhound be sold or found a home, responsibly." Alternative wording put to the authority read as follows:

The greyhound be homed directly on the condition the animal is first neutered and the new home is judged suitable following an independent home check carried out by a representative of the RGT.[9-7]

I suggested further that a maximum fee of £25 plus a capped mileage cost may be charged by the rescue for this service. If I was to look at this again I may tweak the wording slightly but it's not far from what is required. Needless to say, no amendment to the rule has been made. Of course there can never be any guarantees for the future welfare of greyhounds adopted and sadly rescues get it wrong on occasion - sometimes tragically wrong - but what should be in place as an absolute minimum guard is qualified, independent home assessments, made solely with the interest of the dogs in mind.

Greyhounds that fall Boddey's way are in a sense the lucky ones. How many suffer appalling treatment but never attract the attention and help of anyone? Star and Meggie, exhumed from a garden on Allcroft Road, Tyseley (a brief walk from Birmingham's Hall Green track), were starved to death. A further two greyhounds - Pearl and Annie - rescued from the same address weighed only 15.6 and 18 kilos respectively but thankfully survived. The history of all four dogs isn't known but I would be surprised if any had been homed responsibly.

And with the survival of racing increasingly dependent on professional trainers and survival for trainers increasingly dependent on running a large number of dogs there is a need to reduce retirement costs like never before. On just one page of one free-to-post website viewed today seven racing dogs are being advertised free and will end up with God knows whom. Their ages range from two to five, some are mentioned by name, some not. Some are pictured, some not. My fingers are crossed for them but with such ads attracting the wrong kind of people, and trainers wanting retirements out ASAP the odds are not stacked in their favour.

Mistakenidentity: left on his own for 12 hours at a time on most days of the week and found in poor condition

10

Greyhounds in the media

The media by and large cover the court cases, the shock stories and, at the opposite end of the scale, the 'arrh' stories though such coverage it must be said is dwarfed by their promotion of the 'sport'. Nonetheless the media are routinely criticised by members of the racing fraternity who claim cruelty to dogs is only newsworthy when it concerns greyhounds. The truth can be a difficult pill to swallow. I cannot remember the last time a labrador or poodle was found with their ears cut off, the cases of non-greyhounds found shot or dumped in a river with a concrete block attached to their neck are few and far between, and only greyhounds are judged in economic terms and disposed of in their thousands every year when their 'shelf life' has expired. Media coverage has been fair.

That said, media groups are businesses just as the racing industry is a business and the stories making the headlines are the commercially favoured stories. Retired greyhounds Bubbly Totti and Bubbly Pebbles made national news after being *near* starved to death by their owners Andrew and Maria Louden, while Newtown Kerrie *was* starved to death and dumped in a bin but warranted only minimum local media coverage. True, a successful prosecution was brought against the Louden's but more significantly Totti had exchanged hands for £50,000 as a juvenile and went on to win the St Leger. Kerrie on the other hand had never even competed in an 'open'. And frankly some of the media coverage is nothing short of lazy. An article by Guardian columnist Michele Hanson, titled "From the greyhound track to where?" and published 17 March 2010, had more style than substance with figures seemingly plucked from thin air. Yes, it highlighted the racing industry's failure to take proper care of its greyhounds but Hanson's very evident lack of research left it wide open to be discredited by the industry.

Media coverage carries clout and naming and shaming gets results in the reactive-driven world of greyhound racing, and thus discrediting 'anti material' by any means possible is the name of the game. Hanson is simply making it easy for them. Where applicable, racing officials are further quick to discount negative publicity solely on not being up-to-date, and content that is just as relevant today is neither here nor there. In the coverage referenced below I go back no further than 2006 with the majority of stories spanning only the years since the GBGB officially took over the roles of the NGRC and BGRB (1 January 2009). I do not pretend to cover every story but merely provide an insight into aspects of treatment yet to be explored. For historical and contextual purposes I must first though reference the award-winning BBC On the Line exposé "Cradle to grave," aired in January 1994 and instrumental in the birth of GA, and a further comprehensive and damning account of welfare standards in Ireland, published later the same year in The Irish Times.

Ten percent of all runners carrying injuries, 12,000 injuries picked up annually and up to 30,000 greyhounds destroyed every year; just some of the claims made in the BBC programme that raised "serious questions about the ethics of a sport… that is based on the exploitation of animals." Undercover filming exposed the horrendous act of 'feeding' live rabbits to greyhounds - said to make them 'keener' - and former British trainer David Haywood talked about the use of drugs to either affect the animal's performance or mask injuries. Export markets included Spain, and in Valencia the dogs were found in "miserable" conditions, in one-metre square cages and being controlled with the use of rubber hoses. Ultimately, whether it is in Ireland, Britain or elsewhere, most of the dogs faced an untimely death that, as Mark Deane representing the Ulster SPCA explained, was not always humanely carried out: "On a number of times we have found animals which have been clubbed to death; their ears cut off… Household items and cleaners have been used to inject animals."

Issues of welfare on Irish soil were a key element in the programme as Ireland - Northern and the Republic - is inextricably linked to greyhound racing in Britain, primarily in the supply of dogs (75 to 80 percent). It was "feared many thousands are put down before they are twelve months old," and how many of these were bred due to the demand generated by British tracks? Further, ex-racers may return to Ireland. When it comes to breeding and racing, Ireland and Britain are dependent upon each other and for this reason it was important to cover stories from both countries and hence the article referenced above from The Irish Times, titled "Not all dogs go to heaven" (published 24 October 1994).

As in "Cradle to grave" it was taking a broad look at key welfare issues but essentially highlighting a failure on the part of the industry to provide any safety net for the dogs, be they non-graders or otherwise. Britain was slow embracing greyhounds as pets but Ireland was not even out of the starting traps and the very evident absence of older dogs was the telltale sign of an industry with much to hide.

The Cork SPCA has the unenviable task of putting down a number of greyhounds and the busiest days are when the sales are on. Put simply the slow dogs are not wanted and the Society, all too aware of what may happen to them, distributes leaflets encouraging their owners to have the animals destroyed humanely. "Every decision in a greyhound's life is conditioned by economics," reports Louise Coleman of Greyhound Friends. "If it is too slow as a pup it will be put down, if it gets injured while racing it will be similarly discarded and when the dogs get too old to be competitive they are often abandoned, put down, or maybe sent for vivisection."

Universities, medical research laboratories and veterinary schools were all stated as "popular destinations" in the article with Queens University Belfast given specific mention. "One of their experiments signalled the end for 110 greyhounds, the majority of them bought in the Republic." Details of procedures carried out were not given but what we do have is a report by the British Union for the Abolition of Vivisection some five years previously on a specific experiment (said to have taken place at Belfast University):

> In laymen's terms what actually happened was that 119 greyhounds of both sexes were anaesthetised and had either their fourth or fifth rib removed to expose the heart. Wires were then attached [to the] heart and the left coronary artery was tied. The dogs were then allowed to regain consciousness. After 24 hours 32 of the dogs had died. Most suffered strokes, the rest failed to recover from the anaesthetic, haemorrhaged to death or suffered heart failure. Of the 87 dogs who survived the 24-hour period, six were destroyed because of severe wound infections, vomiting and dehydration. Another 15 died 'suddenly and unexpectedly' during the post-operative week. The remainder of the dogs were all given electrical stimulations of the heart via the attached wires.[10-1]

And the Spanish market was again to raise its ugly head. Following previous reports exposing horrific conditions for dogs in Spain, welfare recommendations had supposedly been made and implemented but there was little or no evidence on the ground to support this. Trade agent John Shields countered any criticism of the market by saying: "Some seem to equate Spanish owners with cruelty but even in Ireland I've known many cases where they've had dogs that had been no good and where they've just tied a rope around their necks and thrown them in the river." The trade was certainly indicative of their treatment at home. Dogs kicked out of vehicles returning from race meetings and dogs "bludgeoned to death" or injected with baking soda or brake fluid were other atrocities detailed in The Irish Times. It wasn't the first article of its kind, nor would it be the last. It concluded:

> Greyhound racing is based on the systematic culling of hearty racing dogs which have outlived their usefulness. It is doubtful that the greyhound public is aware that 90 percent of the racers it sees charging towards the line are sent to early graves. It is doubtful too that the great tax-paying public are aware that they are the biggest shareholders in greyhound racing with the government's involvement via Bord na gCon [Irish Greyhound Board].

The Board for their part said they were "proud of the way Irish greyhound owners treat their dogs." Far from me to put words in their mouth but perhaps the response today would be something along the lines 'that was then and this is now'. So what is 'now', beyond what is already covered in this publication - the stories to have gained media attention in more recent years? First is Britain.

Standards in care

In 2008 Peterborough Magistrates' Court heard how seven greyhounds owned by former greyhound trainer Rebecca Hagger "suffered for up to two months in 'squalid conditions' without access to food and water."[10-2] The neglect came to light when in September the previous year the RSPCA visited Red Brick Farm, Fengate, where Hagger first worked as a kennel hand for her late father Frederick. In bloodstained kennels that had an "overpowering stench" of urine and excrement and only small scraps of paper for bedding, seven dogs were found up to six kilos underweight and flea-ridden. Three had numerous pressure sores and lesions. Hagger was banned from keeping animals for 10 years and ordered to do 200 hours community service.

Peterborough track (where Hagger entered runners) is part the regulated sector that requires trainers to kennel dogs. The same does not apply for the independent sector though it is my understanding the majority of dogs *are* kennelled and standards likewise leave much to be desired. At Swansea's flapping track (thankfully now closed) dogs were being kept on site and in less than humane conditions on a visit by environmental health officers in March 2009. The standard of kennels was said "very poor" and specific issues raised included soiled bedding and dim light, "with some kennels in complete darkness."[10-3] Francis Short lived at the track and could boast 55 years experience of greyhound racing but his failure to take proper care of the dogs landed him a fine of £250 plus costs.

At Hillcroft Farm, Frankby, trainer Ian Street kept his greyhounds in a loose-run compound, garden shed and wire kennels said to be "damaged, rusty and bloodstained." A number of the dogs had "severely damaged and bleeding tails, several with old breaks," and coats were reportedly caked in mud, urine and faeces and displaying evidence of heavy flea and mite infestations.[10-4] Wirral Magistrates' Court heard how Street inflicted "terrible suffering" on nearly 30 dogs. Singled out for mention by Kenneth Abraham, prosecuting, was Dancer who had "gingivitis and scabs on her feet," and Tex suffering "complete hair loss on his back half."[10-5] 29 greyhounds were confiscated when the site was raided in April 2009. In February 2010 Street received a four-month jail sentence, suspended for one year, and was banned from keeping animals for life and ordered to pay £1,000 costs.

A similarly harrowing case was heard at Colchester Magistrates' Court in March 2009 and concerned more than 30 greyhounds at kennels in Tiptree, Essex. Robert Freeman had a "partnership" in his father John's "very successful greyhound racing business" and took responsibility for the animals on his father being taken ill. Subsequently, and in what was described as "concentration camp" conditions, greyhounds were left "in cages covered in urine and excrement without food or water for days causing some of them to go 'kennel crazy', biting at the bars and walking round in circles constantly." In response to RSPCA footage of the animals, District Judge David Cooper is reported saying: "Seeing the dogs turn and turn in that way was heartbreaking. It was heedless neglect and cruelty."[10-6] A number of the dogs had untreated injuries and eye problems, many were underweight and flea-ridden. While Freeman, 19, was ordered to serve 90 days in a young offenders' institute, John received a suspended sentence, £500 fine and ordered to pay £2,000 towards the £20,000 costs incurred by the RSPCA. Both were banned from keeping animals for 10 years. 33 dogs were seized.

Thankfully all of the above dogs survived and found new homes but sadly the same could not be said for a number of greyhounds in the 'care' of up-and-coming greyhound breeder Martin Carr. When RSPCA officers visited Carr's Grantham home in March 2011 they discovered four greyhounds starved to death in a garage with a further two suffering "gross neglect," the town's court heard. The emaciated bodies of Sophie and Baby were found in filthy conditions in two pens with little bedding. In another pen Rambo and Secret had died next to each other. Beris Brickles, prosecuting, said: "The two dogs found together had ulcers on their bodies, which suggested they were too weak to stand. They died of starvation, unable to get up at all."[10-7] A further 11 dogs to include seven puppies were found at the property. Two of the dogs, said to be underweight - one severely - and suffering conjunctivitis and dermatitis, were taken away for immediate treatment. The court also heard how the RSPCA had visited Carr on "at least four earlier occasions" which begs the question why these dogs were ever allowed to suffer and die in the way they did.[10-8] Carr received a 90 day suspended sentence and 100 hours community work. Both he and partner Dawn Campbell were banned from keeping animals indefinitely. The Greyhound Stud Book lists a number of entries under either Carr or Carr and Campbell.[10-9]

The number of cases brought before the courts - and so in turn to gain media attention - is, it has to be said, relatively small but if we had in place the resources and will to comprehensively pursue individuals in breach of animal welfare legislation would the justice system have the capacity to cope? I think not. Racing dogs are ultimately viewed as commodities and as such their treatment is driven and ruled by economics. Hanson's article, though in the most part forgettable, did contain one pertinent observation: "As soon as you put humans, animals and money into an equation, you're going to have problems." Nowhere is this better illustrated than in the disposal of greyhounds; a subject that has been a source of rich pickings for the media.

Greyhound disposal

In 2006 the findings of an investigation by The Sunday Times gave a whole new meaning to dogs rescued. Leigh Animal Sanctuary (now renamed), Greater Manchester, was described as a "conveyor belt of killing" and the service provided was, according to one trainer, used by "every track, they come from all over, Belle Vue, Kinsley and Doncaster." The sanctuary, it was reported, charged £35 per dog taken in but the ones judged difficult to home to include greyhounds would get no further than the industrial-sized freezers in "Block 8." Indeed most greyhound trainers/owners "would specially ask for their dogs to be put down."[10-10] The procedure was quick but brutal: lethal drugs fired directly into the animal's chest, and it was claimed a vet was rarely present. The numbers involved allegedly ran into thousands.

Too old, too slow or injured and the most economic route for the greyhound's disposal is sought. In Seaham, County Durham, builders' merchant David Smith was charging a mere £10 and for that you got one dog shot, by way of a bolt gun, and the animal buried on Smith's one-acre plot. It was The Sunday Times first exposé to tear shreds out of racing's glossy exterior and the story the broadsheet is perhaps best remembered for. Etched on peoples memories are the pictures of two bloody and lifeless greyhounds being transported in a wheelbarrow by Smith from his killing shed to their grave. He was cheap and popular. A track insider is reported saying: "Only doing two dogs a day is a bad day for him. It is not unheard of for him to do around 40 a day and if anyone ever digs up that garden it will be like the killing fields." It was estimated that at least 10,000 dogs had suffered the same fate as those captured on film (Smith, of course, has disputed this figure).

It was an episode in the 'sports' more recent history that further did nothing for the reputation of the RSPCA. Debbie Rothery, representing one of the larger greyhound rescues, is quoted saying: "The RSPCA have told me they have not got time to pursue greyhound abusers and parliament does not do anything because they are making too much money from the industry."[10-11] Smith claimed the charity knew of his activity and though he was ultimately put before Durham magistrates it was only in a case brought by the Environment Agency under legislation used to restrict the dumping of waste. He was fined £2,000. "Inquiries by the RSPCA concluded that there was no indication animal cruelty law had been broken."[10-12]

It would be extremely naïve to think Smith was a unique case, and in 2008 The Sunday Times exposed Holts - a knacker's yard in Hertfordshire - for having a "sideline in slaughtering dogs that are no longer fast enough to race." The price was double - £20 - and the dogs were incinerated rather than buried but essentially what was happening was the same; dogs were being killed using a bolt gun and it was a service said by staff carried out for "quite a few trainers" who reportedly visited the yard most weeks. Alan Waller, who runs the company with his partner Jackie, is later confronted and quoted saying: "Greyhound trainers basically just get rid of their dogs when they are no longer any use to them and they can't re-home them. It's just one of the things that happens in an industry where there's too many dogs […] and they can't re-house them all."[10-13]

The above exposé was just one of three by The Sunday Times in 2008; the same year in which BGRB Chairman David Lipsey is reported upbeat on the subject of the dogs' welfare: It is "now well on its way to being resolved […]. You really can't run a modern leisure business if there's any hint of cruelty attached to it. I can now look at myself in the mirror without feeling ashamed, which I couldn't five years ago."[10-14]

Breeder Charles Pickering was never out of the spotlight for too long and not always for reasons he would care to remember. In 2006 the Mail Online reported on a devastating fire to engulf his Zigzag kennels at Dunholme, Lincolnshire, in which more than 30 dogs, brood bitches and puppies lost their lives. Arson was not suspected. In 2010 the Express covered an investigation by a greyhound protection group that filmed dogs "suffering with open wounds and left struggling to find food."[10-15] But it was The Sunday Times exposé from May 2008 that marked the beginning of the end for Pickering. According to the broadsheet, Britain's largest breeder was offering to sell healthy young non-graders to be killed and used for research purposes. The asking price was £30 each for the dogs too slow, not interested in chasing the artificial hare or temperamentally unsuitable for the track. And Pickering is further reported saying that he had been "supplying up to 30 dogs a year to Liverpool University but 'we could do more if required'."[10-16] Later, the story changes and dogs sent to Liverpool are via a trainer named as Richard Fielding and include ex-racers.

Two months prior to the above revelation, Daniel Foggo reported on the killing of healthy greyhounds and sale of their body parts by the Greyhound Clinic in Essex. Based in Ockendon greyhound 'village' - with racing kennels either side, (then) two rescues and a training track - the clinic had a financial agreement with the Royal Veterinary College (RVC) in the provision of organs and charged owners £30 for the disposal of their unwanted greyhounds. The RVC, which admitted having a similar working relationship with other clinics, insisted the animals must be healthy, and sent over representatives once or twice weekly to first extract blood from the dogs before their lives were ended. A quote from the RSPCA read as follows: "We are shocked by this evidence which appears to show an opening for greyhounds to be systematically destroyed for profit. We certainly would not like to think that there was a financial incentive to ending a pet's life."[10-17]

The quote from the RSPCA is welcome but it's time the spokesperson realised greyhounds used for racing are not viewed as pets. If they were, much of the inherent welfare issues within the 'sport' would not exist. When it comes to their disposal the media have identified at least some of the less than savoury individuals or groups operating on a commercial scale (and who would likely still be operating if it was not for their exposure) but many of the dogs are simply abandoned and later picked up and quietly taken in by rescues without the public any the wiser. Their condition varies. It's a scandal not highlighted enough but local media in the most part give mention to a small number.

In what was described as an "horrific and sickening act of cruelty" a greyhound was found on a grass verge in Bedlington, Northumberland, with both ears cut off and electrical tape stuck to his back and legs.[10-18] Removing the dogs' ears is sadly a familiar practice by members of the racing fraternity to prevent identification of the animal from tattoo markings (in both ears for Irish-registered, in the right ear only for British). In the same year, 2009, a further three disturbing cases came to light. A brindle greyhound bitch was picked up in Middlesbrough, emaciated and suffering a wound to her back that was believed caused by some kind of boiling liquid.[10-19] In Kirkcaldy, Fife, a two-year-old greyhound was thrown over the eight foot high perimeter fence of a disused factory and found dehydrated, covered in fleas and weighing just 18 kilos."[10-20] And the condition of a greyhound found near Grimsby Docks, "so weak he had to be carried to a car and taken into immediate care," was the worst seen in 25 years by Sandra Davis of Fen Bank Greyhound Sanctuary.[10-21]

In 2012 two similarly disturbing stories gained media coverage. A "dangerously emaciated" five-year-old greyhound was abandoned at a retail park in Wallsend, Tyne and Wear.[10-22] And in Wigan a former racer with "horrific injuries" was "callously dumped and left for dead." The six-year-old bitch urgently required surgery to include re-attaching muscles to tendons in her back legs. Veterinarian Natalie Oaks is reported saying: "She has raced and made money for someone, it's just a shame they couldn't have taken care of her when she was injured rather than abandoning her, lame and in obvious pain."[10-23] But where greyhounds can be rescued there is hopefully a happy ending. Sadly a small number are found dead and two stories within the space of one week in 2009 made for grim reading.

The body of a brindle greyhound, thought to be about four years old, was discovered close to the village of Trimdon, County Durham. Both ears had been cut off and while the cause of death could not be established a spokesperson for the RSPCA said: "There does appear to be some trauma to the dog's chest."[10-24] The person making the find did not want to be named for fear of reprisals. The other story concerns a black and white greyhound bitch, similar in age and discovered just hours after being dumped in Iron Acton, South Gloucestershire. This poor animal was heavily pregnant with six puppies when killed and again both ears had been cut off.[10-25] You might think it couldn't get any worse but I have yet to cover the atrocities being reported in Ireland. Before I do it's worth reflecting on the stories above and the fact that it was not in the nineties that greyhound racing was established in Britain but rather the twenties, and that since 2007 the animals have 'enjoyed' greater protection by way of the Animal Welfare Act 2006 and the Animal Health and Welfare (Scotland) Act 2006, both incorporating a duty of care. Better protection would seemingly exist only on paper.

Ireland

There may not be an immediate and glaring difference in what the Irish press report but take a closer look and what is noticeable, unfortunately by its absence, are successful prosecutions brought against trainers, owners or breeders but do not think this in anyway is a reflection of how the animals are treated. With Ireland big on breeding and decades behind Britain in viewing greyhounds as anything other than commodities much of the media coverage concerns their disposal - humane or otherwise. It is a sad reflection on the IGB and, dare I say, the Irish people that greyhounds have to be exported - to countries such as the Czech Republic - to be adopted, though wonderful also that at least a small number can be. Quoted in The Irish Times is founder of Czech group Greathounds In Need, Lucie Poucova: "This industry makes so much money but puts hardly anything into caring for dogs when they retire. The Irish Greyhound Board does not operate a single shelter and most owners don't want to spend money on dogs when they stop racing." As for the scale of retirements the Board's Welfare Manager, Barry Coleman, is reported saying: "Those figures are not available."[10-26]

The article further highlighted the number of greyhounds put down by Irish pounds in 2010 - 822 taken in and 672 destroyed (see table below for a breakdown covering 2010 and 2011) - and the discrepancy between breeding and adoption figures that left thousands of greyhounds unaccounted for. In June 2012 and three months following its publication The Irish Mail on Sunday carried a moving story on the pound in Ennis, operated by Clare County Council with the Irish SPCA. The owners are given a one-hour window every Friday to bring their greyhounds in, and within one hour the dogs are killed. A fee of €20 is charged. The policy - not limited to Clare or ISPCA pounds - is driven, according to the charity, by a fear the dogs would otherwise be abandoned and the fact "Irish people just have not embraced greyhounds as pets."[10-27]

Irish pound statistics 2010-11

Pound	Greyhounds taken in - 2010	PTS	taken in - 2011	PTS
Carlow	6	3	5	2
Cavan	4	4	2	2
Clare	202	202	147	147
Cork City	9	3	6	1
Cork County	45	45	22	16
Donegal	45	45	37	37
Dublin City	18	0	3	1
Dún Laoghaire/Rathdown	5	0	9	0
Fingal	5	0	2	0
Galway City	36	36	38	38
Galway County	3	0	5	0
Kerry	150	114	99	72
Kildare	5	5	7	4
Kilkenny	6	4	7	3
Laois	9	1	7	0
Leitrim	3	0	2	0
Limerick City	3	3	5	5
Limerick County	66	58	63	59
Longford	7	5	11	10
Louth	20	12	16	8
Mayo	1	0	0	0
Meath	9	2	28	3
Monaghan	6	2	6	0
North Tipperary	17	14	7	7
Offaly	33	30	0	0
Roscommon	7	7	10	10
Sligo	5	0	8	2
South Dublin	14	0	21	4
South Tipperary	22	22	62	62
Waterford City	4	4	1	0
Waterford County	4	2	3	1
Westmeath	45	45	52	52
Wexford	0	0	0	0
Wicklow	8	4	9	0

The ISPCA are also very aware of the kind of ill treatment inflicted on greyhounds to be abandoned. A greyhound bitch found in Banbridge, County Down, had part of one ear mutilated and her legs bound. She was described as "no more than a bag of bones."[10-28] And in Tramore, County Waterford, a greyhound with both ears missing was found wandering the streets "hungry, thirsty and terrified." Such was her anxiety around people it took six hours to capture the young dog, subsequently named Aoife. As for her injuries, Andrew Quinn representing Waterford SPCA, is reported saying: "The first cut was very sudden and took one ear cleanly off, but the second, well, all I can say is that she put up some fight."[10-29]

The above are far from unique cases but the media were to follow the story of Aoife for more than a year. A DNA sample was taken from the dog to help identify her and hopefully, in turn, the person responsible for the savage attack. It was the first time within the above context the IGB had used DNA profiling and Aoife's registered owner was identified but no action was taken for lack of evidence, apparently. Quinn's anger was aimed firmly at racing's governing body: "At first the IGB was all over this and they rushed in to take a hair sample and get statements but over the past year [the Board] has cooled off and show no intention of bringing someone to book. I don't blame the gardai [police] as I don't think the IGB gave them enough to go on."[10-30]

I understand both dogs made a good recovery. Characteristic of media coverage for Ireland are the reports of greyhounds found dead that are far greater in number than is the case in Britain. The bodies of five badly decomposed dogs were washed up onto Kilmore Strand, County Kerry, late in 2006. It was difficult simply identifying the breed but the gardai investigating were under the assumption the dogs were all greyhounds.[10-31] In 2008 the carcasses of several dogs discovered in woodland near Coppeen, County Cork, prompted fears the isolated area was a dumping ground for unwanted greyhounds.[10-32] And later the same year The Irish Times ran a story on the bodies of two greyhounds, estimated no more than about three years of age, plucked from a tributary of the river Foyle in County Donegal. The ears of one of the dogs - a male - had been cut off and there was rope around the neck of the other - a female - indicating a weight was originally attached to the dog. Irish SPCA inspector Kevin McGinley dealt with the find and is reported saying: "People who are capable of doing something like this to animals could be just as capable of human abuse."[10-33]

Similar cases made the headlines in 2009. In what was described as "the tip of the iceberg" a greyhound carcass was washed-up along the bank of the river Foyle in a suburb of Derry. The dog, trussed up in a potato sack before being tossed into the river, made an "ill-fated fight for survival" and forced his/her hind legs through the sack but was unable to escape.[10-34] Moving south the remains of three greyhounds were discovered in the area of Kilteery Pier on the Shannon Estuary. The ears of all dogs had been cut off.[10-35] Despite such gruesome finds, Coleman - the IGB's Welfare Manager - "does not accept that there is a problem with neglect, or that the current practice of tattooing animals can lead to dogs' ears being hacked off to prevent identification." The brutality is there for all to see but perhaps Coleman has some other idea as to motive? Cosmetic?

The quote is taken from a compelling article in the Irish Daily Mail that was to highlight the plight of greyhounds in the light of new breeding legislation opposed by the IGB. It concluded by quoting Marion Fitzgibbon, former president of the Irish SPCA: "If a labrador or any other breed of dog was treated as appallingly as greyhounds are in this country, there would be complete outrage. My American, German, Italian and English friends can't believe how we treat the greyhound. It makes me very ashamed to be Irish."[10-36]

Fitzgibbon's sentiment would likely be shared by two recreational divers who, early in 2011, discovered two greyhounds on the seabed off Garron Point on the Antrim coast. The dogs were being held down in eight metres of water by concrete blocks attached to the animals by way of rope. Alan Ward, representing the Ulster SPCA, said it was the view of the charity the animals were still alive when disposed of. He added: "I think it would have been a terrible death for those dogs, we can just picture them underneath the water with rope around their necks trying to escape to the surface for air. It's a barbaric act to carry out on any animal."[10-37]

During the Easter weekend, 2012, yet another gruesome discovery was made, on this occasion by a person walking their dog near the village of Ballyagran, County Limerick. The walker had inadvertently stumbled across a number of greyhounds in varying stages of decomposition in a disused local quarry. Inspection of the site revealed at least seven dogs strewn amongst dense vegetation, to include two born only the previous year. Fitzgibbon visited the site and is reported saying: "The smell is absolutely unbearable. They appear to have been shot because you can see all the blood on the green, and then thrown down into the pit." Indeed examination of the animals revealed shooting was the cause of death and owners were soon identified via the dogs' ear markings. "We are giving very strong assurances to the public that the perpetrators of this awful act will be pursued and [...] face the full rigours of the law," said Coleman at the time, but a prosecution was brought only against one person - John Corkery - for irregularities in paperwork for two of the dogs found (Rathluirc Sham and Kildangan Dawn) and nothing more.[10-38]

And it should come as no surprise that Ireland too had its knacker-men serving the industry, or as the Irish Sun chose to put it: "Owners are paying less than the price of a ticket to a night at the dogs to have off-the-pace greyhounds gunned down." Larry Earle, it was claimed, charged €10 per dog for the service he provided at his Camolin based business, County Wexford. The weapon used is again the bolt gun. Earle could not say how many greyhounds he had killed but hinted farmers too are shooting the dogs for cash. Pragmatic dismay might best sum up a quote from Chief Inspector Conor Dowling of the Irish SPCA: "One of the unfortunate consequences of greyhound breeding is that a large number of dogs don't make the grade and are often unwanted. [...]. It is unfortunate that some people prefer to take the cheaper, easier way out."[10-39] It's that mix of humans, animals and money that Hanson speaks of, and in 2011 the IGB were likely rubbing their hands with glee at the prospect of a multi-million euro deal with China, but at what cost to the greyhounds?

Ireland in China

It is a grim picture for greyhounds in Ireland, of that there is no question, but not as grim as it is for dogs exported to China; a country where the most basic animal welfare protection and provision is lacking and where, it has been shown, dogs are brutally slaughtered for human consumption and fur. Yet this was a country the IGB were looking to establish a business venture with. What the Board had misjudged, however, was public reaction. The story broke in February 2011 and left no doubt in anyone's minds about the industry's priorities (for that reason it is relevant to cover here). Exporting greyhounds to China was just one part of an "international expansion that could result in it [the IGB] operating racing stadiums there," reported The Sunday Times. Chinese officials had visited Dublin the same month and viewed how the industry is operated and the Board had informed the Department of Agriculture of their expansion plans. On welfare the Board is reported saying: "We do not have any influence on the welfare standards adopted in other countries, and these matters are more appropriately dealt with by the country's own legislative system."[10-40]

In a letter on behalf of the Dogs Trust, Dublin SPCA, Irish SPCA and Irish Blue Cross, the response was swift and unequivocal: "This venture is being pursued with no consideration for the welfare of greyhounds. The future of Irish greyhounds in China would at best be short lived and at worst dire and unthinkable."[10-41] Demonstrations were held in Dublin, Edinburgh and London, opposition was mounting worldwide and suddenly the IGB became all welfare minded, but assurances of "absolute control and integrity within a strong welfare framework" carried little weight with opponents: "Anyone familiar with the Board's abysmal record in relation to its responsibility to raced greyhounds in Ireland would find the reassurances hollow in the extreme," said Bernie Wright of Greyhound Action Ireland.[10-42]

In May 2011 it was reported in The Irish Times that the Department of Agriculture had refused to approve a proposal from the IGB to export Irish greyhounds to China. A victory of a sort but in the view of IGB Chief Executive, Adrian Neilan, there remained "a great business opportunity" and the change would allow the Board to focus on that area of the project requiring "our expertise in the design, build and subsequent long-term management of brand-new stadia in China."[10-43]

The reality is dogs would likely be imported from Australia instead, as is the case for China's one legal track: the Canidrome in Macau. Could this serve as a blueprint for a new greyhound industry in China? The Irish Daily Mail travelled to Macau to take a closer look and found that for the dogs it is a one-way-ticket. 800 are kept on site in metal cages stacked two high and offering barely enough room to turn around in. Every month about 30 new dogs are brought in and about 30 are killed. Not a single one will leave the track alive and three years is the best the dogs can hope for. In 2010, 383 were destroyed due to a drop in their performance or injuries sustained on the track. "This is greyhound racing Chinese-style," writes the Mail, and "this is the depressingly cruel industry Ireland's greyhound racing authority, Bord na gCon [Irish Greyhound Board], controversially wants to expand to cities across China."[10-44]

Mercifully, in 2012, the permission the Board required from the Department of Agriculture to proceed with its ambitious plans was refused. An insight into their decision was provided by way of information obtained under the Freedom of Information Act and published in the Independent: The plan "does not provide sufficient assurance that adequate provision would be made to safeguard the health and welfare of greyhounds in China at the end of their racing life."[10-45]

It's incredible to think that any group or individual would even consider exporting greyhounds to China, but then again this was a "compelling" business opportunity in the view of the Board. Do not expect the hand dealt greyhounds in Ireland to improve markedly until it makes good business sense to do so.

11

Measuring greyhounds killed

That many greyhounds are killed, including ex-racers, there is no doubt but what are the figures - exact figures, that is, for each year? I don't know and the industry doesn't know but they should. If the industry had its priorities the correct way round a system would be in place accounting for every single greyhound, though such information would never be published. Of course we have a good idea of how many across the British Isles are disposed of every year; we need only look at the number of greyhounds being bred annually (see table below) and allow for a relatively very small number being kept by their owners and/or used for breeding.

Year (1 June-31 May)	*NCC litters	Puppies (litters x 6.3)	Year	*ICC litters	Puppies (litters x 6.3)	Total
2000-2001	696	4385	2001	3867	24362	28747
2001-2002	788	4964	2002	4565	28760	33724
2002-2003	908	5720	2003	4611	29049	34769
2003-2004	857	5399	2004	4228	26636	32035
2004-2005	707	4454	2005	4366	27506	31960
2005-2006	690	4347	2006	4318	27203	31550
2006-2007	571	3597	2007	4038	25439	29036
2007-2008	531	3345	2008	3819	24060	27405
2008-2009	462	2911	2009	3165	19940	22851
2009-2010	412	2596	2010	3003	18919	21515
2010-2011	340	2142	2011	3272	20614	22756
2011-2012	312	1966	2012	2980	18774	20740

*NCC: covering predominantly British litters. June to May figures are given simply because that is how they are recorded in the Greyhound Stud Book. ICC: covering predominantly Irish litters.

The table highlights a welcome fall year on year in the number of greyhounds bred across the British Isles for the period 2003 to 2010 (34769>21515), dropping by more than 38 percent. Looking solely at NCC figures the fall (in percentage terms) is significantly greater: more than 65 percent between 2003 and 2012.

An understanding of the number of greyhounds killed can be gained by comparing above figures with homing figures though as with so much to do with greyhound racing it is not quite that simple. If, as is the case in this exercise, we are seeking to ascertain numbers in relation to greyhound racing in Britain we next have to establish how many greyhounds are being bred due to the demand generated by British tracks and how many of these dogs, realistically, are being homed (responsibly or otherwise).

As previously covered in "Thousands of greyhound puppies unaccounted for" it is the racing industry in Britain and Ireland that fuels the breeding of virtually all litters recorded with the NCC and ICC, with the export market predominately one way: NCC registered puppies competing on home soil and ICC registrations for the home market and export (Britain by and large). The number of races held and not the number of tracks can best measure the size of the 'sport' - or at least its size relevant to how many greyhounds are bred - and Britain stages more than three times the number of races held in Ireland. About 20,000 being staged annually on Irish soil, whereas in Britain the number for the regulated sector is hovering close to 60,000 nowadays. Include the independent meetings and the total is nearer 70,000. Based on a ratio of 1:3 the numbers of greyhounds bred due to the demand generated by the British greyhound racing industry is as follows:

Year	Puppies	Year	Puppies	Year	Puppies
2001	21560	2005	23970	2009	17138
2002	25293	2006	23663	2010	16136
2003	26077	2007	21777	2011	17067
2004	24026	2008	20554	2012	15555

On dogs homed there are official figures for greyhounds adopted through the RGT and these are for any earmarked greyhounds, be they non-graders or ex-racers, having competed on regulated or independent tracks. We do not, however, have anything other than an estimate for dogs homed via other rescues and independently by their owners/trainers with the figure, as already mentioned, of 3,500 given in a report for the Greyhound Forum. This being the industry's own estimate it is hardly to fall short of the true number, and call me cynical but after many years conducting research into greyhound welfare I have good reason to question information published by industry officials and would happily include in the above figure dogs kept by their owners/trainers. It may still be on the generous side.

Sadly, and likely as much to do with the economic recession as anything else, figures for the RGT have declined significantly since the record number of 4,725 for 2009. It would I believe be reasonable to assume the industry's best estimate for other dogs homed reflects previous and subsequent RGT numbers though I remember a discussion with the then Trust's Executive Director, Ivor Stocker, who at least would not dispute the notion put to him that increased efforts on the part of the Trust to home more dogs was at the 'expense' of other rescue associations lacking the money to advertise or throw in lots of freebies to include collar, lead, muzzle and coat. If true, I don't know how it could be factored in and the table below simply gives RGT numbers and estimates for their counterparts based on the figure of 3,500 given by the industry and the fluctuation in Trust figures.

| Year | Rescued/retained: | | Total | Year | Rescued/retained: | | Total |
	RGT	Other			RGT	Other	
2001	1893	1479	3372	2007	4479	3500	7979
2002	2030	1586	3616	2008	4578	3577	8155
2003	2608	2038	4646	2009	4725	3692	8417
2004	3001	2345	5346	2010	4247	3319	7566
2005	3433	2682	6115	2011	4120	3220	7340
2006	3920	3063	6983	2012	3910	3056	6966

While the totals are based in part on estimates and there is a question mark concerning less recent RGT official numbers (see p. 35) these figures are likely the most realistic published to date. Another set of statistics yet covered and commonly referenced solely against homing figures by the industry (it looks good but is highly misleading: more on that later) are the annual registrations for dogs to compete within the regulated sector. Such registrations are useful in establishing data on the scale of non-graders but are largely academic in understanding the total number of greyhounds unaccounted for. They are, however, very relevant in that the majority of dogs killed are non-graders. For that reason they are included in the table below that compares, side-by-side, the key figures established in relation to greyhound racing in Britain.

Year	Dogs bred (to meet British demand)	Rescued/retained	Track registrations (regulated sector)
2001	21560	3372	9895
2002	25293	3616	10722
2003	26077	4646	10709
2004	24026	5346	11912
2005	23970	6115	11412
2006	23663	6983	10101
2007	21777	7979	9751
2008	20554	8155	9012
2009	17138	8417	8672
2010	16136	7566	8552
2011	17067	7340	7972
2012	15555	6966	7964

Comparing dogs rescued/retained against the corresponding breeding figure we see a dramatic fall in the number of greyhounds unaccounted for and presumed killed, from 21,677 (25,293 - 3,616) (2002) to 8,570 (16,136 - 7,566) (2010) but, disturbingly, a subsequent reversal in this trend. I have avoided including an additional column highlighting the disparity in both sets of figures because the ultimate fate of all dogs bred in any one 12-month period will span many years from puppies judged not fit for purpose to runners not retiring until five (plus) years of age. Research indicates about 30 percent of dogs adopted are non-graders. If making comparisons with track registrations it's further important to bear in mind most dogs are not *competing* until about one-and-a-half years young and retire when about three-and-a-half, to four.

Of course the above is flawed. A small number of Irish dogs never exported to Britain do find homes and these will include dogs bred to meet the demand generated by British tracks and perhaps ultimately adopted in countries to include the Netherlands, France, Belgium, Germany, Italy and the Czech Republic. Indeed the IGB's Welfare Manager, Barry Coleman, is on record saying: "While the rates of adoption in Ireland are growing, 99 percent of greyhounds are re-homed to the continent."[11-1] Numbers are, however, pitifully low. "If you total the number we re-home abroad and those we financially assist to re-home here we have re-homed 530 dogs to the end of November," reported Coleman in December 2011, adding: "It was 680 last year and we hope to hit that total again."[11-2] Further, racing in Britain will account for very few of these dogs when you consider the prospect for non-graders is dire to say the least.

It's flawed also in that breeding figures given in relation to greyhound racing in Britain do not take into account all markets for Irish bred dogs to include hare coursing and exports further afield, e.g. America, mainland Europe, Australia and Pakistan; marginal though they are (on this subject it's worthy of note many of the Irish dogs competing outside the British Isles do so following a career in Ireland, or Ireland and Britain, complicating the picture further).[11-3] The ratio of 1:3 used in calculations made is though generous (compensating at least in part for other markets). No system in accounting for all greyhounds is perfect but frankly nothing can explain the massive disparity between the number of greyhounds bred and how many are likely adopted or kenneled for the remainder of their lives when of no further use for racing.

The fluctuations in annual figures makes same year comparisons misleading but comparisons have to be made and comparing dogs bred against track registrations one year on and rescued/retained figures three years on should in theory be *less* misleading. Perhaps comparisons are best made using mean figures spanning a number of years. Such figures covering a five year period are as follows:

Years	Dogs bred (to meet British demand)	Rescued/retained	Track registrations (regulated sector)
2008-2012	86450	38444	42172
Annual mean figure	17290	7689	8434

Track registrations are of course just that; not all dogs registered will reach competition stage. It's a grim picture and worse than figures might suggest. What kind of life do many of the rescued or retained dogs have? No life at all if the dogs remain kenneled in retirement as is the case for a small number retained by their trainer owners. It was a subject touched on by RGT co-ordinator Amanda Ainsworth:

> I firmly believe in quality of life above all else. Simply keeping an animal alive is not good enough though that principal applies to all living things, including people. I personally would not want to live out my days in misery or great discomfort and I wouldn't subject my pets to a similar fate. […]. Greyhounds need to be loved and cherished. I have known of numerous cases where older dogs have been well fed and kept healthy, but they have spent long hours on their beds in a racing kennel. They can become institutionalised, particularly if they don't have an owner to give them a walk and the staff don't have time. […]. We don't home dogs because it is cheaper than keeping them in kennels. We home them because it is what makes them happiest and gives them the most fulfilling life after racing.[11-4]

Ainsworth was expressing her "own personal views, and not RGT policy." More could be said. What about the greyhounds kenneled for life and not kept healthy? One such dog came to my attention more recently; a long since ex-racer that in her twilight years (and no thanks to her trainer/owner) was 'rescued' from a miserable kennel existence. The greyhound was suffering both worms and fleas, her mouth was severely infected and 23 teeth had to be removed. Other issues included significant hair loss on her back and hind legs.

"We recently brought home our ex-racer," writes another owner, but that new home was again a kennel and the dog was barking and upsetting the neighbours. A strap muzzle was obtained for the dog but advice was also being sought in the Greyhound Star on other methods to 'cure' the problem. Recommended was a collar that delivers an electric shock "if he appears to enjoy barking."[11-5] What life does this poor greyhound have? What life do many of the dogs being indiscriminately homed by their trainers/owners have? The 'perfect pet' advertising of these dogs and ease in which not just their trainers/owners off-load them should be of concern to anyone whose interest is solely the welfare of the animals.[11-6]

We can only surmise what the disparity is in the number of greyhounds bred and the number of non-graders/ex-racers receiving a good quality of life. The table above is reason enough to question the very existence of greyhound racing. Yes, figures demonstrate an encouraging move in the right direction but that has as much to do with track closures and the subsequent drop in races held as it does in the rise of dogs adopted/kept, and very recent figures suggest any further reduction in the number of greyhounds unaccounted for and presumed killed will at best be marginal unless we see a further and significant decline in meetings staged. Yes, there are flaws in the calculations made but even allowing for this it would be fair to assume the number of dogs being prematurely killed has not fallen below about 50 percent. In recent years and based on the mean figures given above, the annual total was 9,500 thereabouts. And what of the number since the first meeting was staged at Belle Vue back in 1926? There are many factors to consider but it would be naïve in the extreme to think it didn't far exceed one million.

12

Defending the indefensible

So we have an industry in which there exists widespread exploitation and abuse of its core product - essentially a betting product - namely the greyhound. There exists repeated violation of animal welfare legislation, the quality of life for racing dogs leaves much to be desired, the number of injuries sustained annually competing on the dangerously configured tracks is catastrophic, hundreds of greyhounds are put down every year as a result of injury - on humane or economic grounds - and thousands are denied the chance of adoption when their value as commodities expires.

It would reasonable to question how the industry survives in 21st century 'caring' Britain, particularly when you consider the damaging media attention it has received in more recent years and the substantial cash return - generated from public support - needed to keep going. Desperate times calls for desperate measures and various tactics are employed to include intimidation, scaremongering, the circulation of misleading or simply inaccurate information, the withholding of information (on a level that would shame MI6), desperate promotional ventures, supporting good causes, promoting a seemingly healthy working relationship with national animal welfare charities and of course maintaining its self-regulating status (as recommended in the 'independent' review of the industry by Lord Donoughue of Ashton).

RGT co-ordinator Amanda Ainsworth has stated: "If we are absolutely honest, the vast majority of the public are indifferent to greyhound racing one way or another. At either end of the scale are people for and against."[12-1] Wrong, wrong, wrong! And the industry does not view it that way. I do not pretend for one moment we are a nation of animal lovers but most people, while not wishing to hold up 'you bet, they die' banners outside race meetings, would not wish to support the racing knowing it has failed the dogs. A point not lost on former BGRB Chairman, David Lipsey: "The sport realises that its customers, whether in betting shops or on track, have to be confident that it cares for its canine competitors or they will withdraw their patronage."[12-2] Ainsworth's boss, Peter Laurie, said something very similar some eight years on. Of course there is reality and perceived reality and without the latter the industry might now be hooked up to a life-support machine.

The quote from Lipsey further highlights another tactic employed: selling the betting product as a sport. It is though an activity not recognised by Sport England, Sport Northern Ireland, Sport Scotland, Sport Wales and UK Sport. The sports' councils together observe a definition of sport laid down by the Council of Europe's European Sports Charter 1993, and among the broad spectrum of activities to gain recognition are caving, darts and arm wrestling but not greyhound racing. The GBGB can call it what they like but officially it is not recognised as a sport; a point lost on the BBC when Drumcove Lad - 2011 Sprinter of the Year - appeared as the mystery guest on A Question of Sport, no doubt to the delight of industry officials.

It was a great promotional opportunity, the like of which is seemingly needed where tactics to get people through the turnstiles had resorted to free entry and giving meals away. Actually that is not strictly true, punters were given free entry and a meal for one penny in a promotion that covered 22 of Britain's regulated tracks (one can only speculate about the 'dining experience'). The theory is it would introduce new people to greyhound racing though how successful it has been (in generating new income) isn't known.

More recently the Big Dog Tour was grabbing the headlines. Looking like something that had escaped from Blackpool seafront, a stretched limousine topped with a giant racing greyhound embarked on a tour of the regulated sector from Monmore, Wolverhampton, in October 2011. "Anything that can get people to come racing can only be a good thing," was the reported view of the track's deputy racing manager Tony Williamson.[12-3] Of course it was given a positive spin in the GBGB Annual Report (2011) and for sure it will have turned many people's heads (both motorists and pedestrians (let's hope it didn't cause any serious accidents)) but in January 2013 it was announced funding for 'Big Dog' would cease following apparent divided opinion on its marketing value. Harlow boss Dave Barclay was not too impressed: "I keep reading that it is has been a huge success yet here we have only had eight free admission tickets handed in and it has cost the industry way into six figures."[12-4]

I sympathise, well at least appreciate, the difficulty selling greyhound racing to a nowadays-more-aware British public. It would be a headache for the greatest of marketing gurus and all the more reason to stifle any information that may present further hurdles in marketing the 'sport' to a new audience. In this area the racing industry excels. In this area there must be many a red face: "Worried about feeding the antis? Wouldn't you be more embarrassed to be in an industry with issues that might need to be hidden?"[12-5]

A number of years back when first getting involved in the whole welfare debate my focus was Yarmouth stadium and collating data on the fate of dogs that retired off the track and, more specifically, the number of dogs put down following injury; information that should be held by the regulator. I contacted the then NGRC Retired Greyhound Co-ordinator Luke Taylor and was told the information sought could not be provided due to the Data Protection Act. Really? According to the Information Commissioner's Office the information in question was (surprise, surprise) not covered by the Act.[12-6] I next spoke with NGRC Security Co-ordinator Noel

Thompson who perhaps wasn't accustomed to direct questions on sensitive issues and was clearly unprepared (the image of rabbit caught in headlights came to mind). Could Thompson provide information on dogs no-longer running? Apparently not, and the chief reason given you might just be able to decipher in the following response:

> If I believe or there is a possibility that some innocent party could be injured or hurt or in some way as a result of certain information going out, innocent information going out, erm, of this nature then I would be very concerned of passing that information on. And that's why anybody is guarded because anything in the world there are, erm, people who are, erm, anti all sorts of things. Now there are some people that are, erm, and quite rightly so, they voice their concerns that they don't like greyhound racing, people voice their concerns that they don't like horse racing.[12-7]

Similar requests made in writing to the GBGB have been ignored. The reality is much information concerning the fate of racing dogs could, if in the public domain, prove damaging for the *business* of greyhound racing. Likewise details more specifically concerning the frequency and nature of injuries sustained on the track; a subject that remains one of the most sensitive and guarded within racing, though its concealment carries little if any support outside their own ranks. Publication of such information was a key recommendation in the APGAW report on the welfare of greyhounds in England:

> We recommend that the greyhound industry should be required by law under statutory regulations to record and publish annual injuries to greyhounds on a central database. The regulatory body of the greyhound industry should publish an annual report to include three-year rolling averages for injury incidence at named tracks. This report should also include information about how the track has attempted to reduce the injury rate.[12-8]

DEFRA addressed the subject some two years later, favouring publication of data on a voluntary basis and anonymised:

> It is important that the sole industry governing body, the GBGB, commits itself to publishing anonymised, aggregate [injury] data collected from its tracks. […]. We understand that the requirement for a new, comprehensive injury database is enshrined in the company's Memorandum and Articles of Association. It is our expectation that the GBGB will give serious

consideration to the publication of anonymous, aggregate data from this database to further demonstrate that it is an open and transparent body.[12-9]

The strength of feeling for publication of such data was made abundantly clear in the responses given to a question (#23) in the government's consultation on the Welfare of Racing Greyhounds Regulations 2010 that merely asked "do you agree that tracks should be required to keep injury records?" A large number of the 307 respondents (groups and individuals), whether agreeing or disagreeing on where/how records are held, felt the information should be in the public domain. A further 1,694 respondents to include 1,671 private individuals "called separately for injury rates to be published."[12-10] It was one of the largest responses to any question posed in the consultation.

As already mentioned the RCPA compile and hold a database on track injuries that, while limited only to the regulated sector and those injuries indentified and recorded at the time of racing/trials, is the largest database of its kind. On a number of occasions since July 2007 I have contacted the association about access to this information, and the response given was always the same; at some point in the future it will be made available to the public but we cannot say when and in what form. Six years on and the climate of secrecy prevails.

In the APGAW report, Lipsey's justification for withholding such information echoes Thompson's spurious mutterings: "We cannot and will not contemplate publishing data for named individual tracks. To do so would be to risk extremist attacks on tracks and those that work on them." It says much about the content but why not the publication of anonymised data? The report expressed "doubts about the validity of the argument."[12-8]

To gain some understanding on the industry's position and what is being concealed we need only look at data compiled by GREY2K USA - the largest greyhound protection organisation in the USA. The group has had a degree of success (as well as difficulty) in obtaining documents detailing injuries racing dogs have suffered at a number of tracks in America that, as in Britain, are oval-like in configuration. Between 1 January 2007 and 3 November 2009, 923 injuries were *reported* for Tucson Greyhound Park and Phoenix Greyhound Park in Arizona. At Phoenix (where operations ceased in December 2009) the mean monthly figure was 21. A breakdown of the findings are as follows: fractures 44 percent, sprains 17 percent, muscle tears and strains 14 percent, lacerations 7 percent, dislocations 5 percent and others (to include amputation, nerve injury, paralysis and puncture wounds) 13 percent. Broken legs accounted for 249 of the injuries. The following are examples of comments given in the records obtained by GREY2K USA from the Arizona Department of Racing:

- "Fractured right intertarsal joints, broken hock, right rear, recommend x-rays/surgical repair, decided on euthanasia." Injury Report for Bocs Flamingo, 12 August 2009

- "Euthanasia - fractured spine." Injury Report for Figs Speckles, 9 May 2009

- "Broken skull - laceration with brain coming out! DOA - no treatment." Injury Report for Oxbow Savage, 11 April 2009

- "Collision with dog, ran into #5 going into 1st turn, fell, run over, compound fracture left radius and ulna, badly broken [PTS]." Injury Report for Lovin Spoonful, 17 February 2009

- "Fracture right front leg, severely shattered, trainer requested euthanasia." Injury Report for Red I Secret, 15 January 2009

- "Dog hit fence, lots of blood [puncture, abrasion and rupture left carpus]." Injury Report for Mullroy, 20 January 2008

- "Euthanised due to broken hock, young pup just schooling in 2nd career race." Injury Report for Survivor Dog, 10 September 2007

- "Back injury, no feeling rear legs/tail [PTS]." Injury Report for Too Tall Sky, 23 February 2007

- "Broken back out of start box, fracture and bilateral paralysis of rear legs, put down at track." Injury Report for Be Bop Tango, 8 January 2007

It should come as no surprise that "since November 2009, the Arizona Department of Racing has denied multiple public information requests for additional injury data."[12-11] Likewise in Britain it is not the kind of material you want in the public domain. Witnessing a greyhound in unimaginable distress and/or pain is not conducive to birthday celebrations, a hen party or whatever else the occasion is and the chances are, at any one of the meetings staged on British soil, greyhounds will be injured. The thesis by Brian Agnew (see p. 41) highlights an incident rate per meeting for the old Perry Barr track of 2.2. Even according to NGRC estimates given in a more recent government public consultation document, "about two injured dogs were treated on-site per race meeting on NGRC tracks. The nature of injuries is variable and ranges from minor skin trauma to fracture requiring fixation or injuries requiring euthanasia."[12-12]

The GBGB annual report for 2009, however, boasts a "third successive year of comprehensive investment in track safety," and projects to include the installation of track drainage systems, new running rails, camber adjustments and supply of modern track preparation equipment "designed to reduce the incidence of injuries."[12-13] Similar work is detailed in the group's 2010 and 2011 reports. The Board's track safety consultant, John Haynes, claimed in the Greyhound Star (June 2011) the injury rate has, through the improvement in track conditions, been reduced by more than 20 percent but this is seemingly at odds with the experience of many at grass roots' level. Of course no data has been published to support this claim.

Much of what the industry has to say via the media verges on the ludicrous. In a debate surrounding the proposal for a new track in Liverpool back in 2003, a GRA spokesman countered criticism of the track's tight configuration by stating that a larger radius than the 42 metres proposed will "put the dogs in greater danger because they would run faster on a larger track." He further described the criticism as "uninformed."[12-14] You couldn't make it up! Equally absurd is the defence given by Towcester Racecourse in relation to a new track that was set to open at the venue in 2013 and which, we are told, "was designed in a way that would not harm competing dogs."[12-15] It is remarkable how the 'new kids on the block' have created the first *safe* oval-like configured track in the history of greyhound racing. Unfortunately the media print this stuff and I suspect a large proportion of the readership believe it.

Spouting drivel, knowingly or otherwise (I guess Towcester has been fed a diet of manure from the outset of this new venture), runs parallel with the sometimes extraordinary lengths the industry will go to in concealing the hazardous nature of greyhound racing. In February 2008, all members of Greyhoundscene - the largest online forum for the UK racing fraternity - were being warned (via the private messaging facility) about GA; it was stated the group were picking out posts concerning greyhounds put down following injury on the track. Of course they were right but much of the information obtained by GA came straight from the horse's mouth and not any website. In October 2008, a new thread raising awareness about the "odd" phone calls was posted. There are people contacting "trainers to find out about injuries to dogs," wrote Donna Scase, adding "please don't answer them, this goes for any trainer/owner as these people are causing havoc."[12-16] Trainers were certainly increasingly suspicious of any calls made, and postings highlighting fatalities, though only ever occasional (for obvious reasons), were diminishing in number. Nonetheless, in July 2010 it was felt necessary to again warn members about the posting of such information.

Whatever the nature of posts and whoever the author, if judged potential ammunition for the antis it is unlikely to remain on the internet. The newly formed GOBATA, perhaps naïvely, expressed in their online news' column concerns "over what appears to be an inordinate amount of injuries currently being suffered by greyhounds all over the country. [...], too many of them career-threatening broken hocks."[12-17] Communication with the Society of Greyhound Veterinarians (SGV) and champion trainer Mark Wallis was covered in the stories and group chairman Martin White was looking to the GBGB to "advise practitioners of the actual figures" and for data comparisons from previous years (not even trainers and owners have access to the RCPA databank).[12-18] The GOBATA posting is exactly what you would expect from an open and transparent industry but within days, if not hours, of (myself) speaking with the regulator about the content it was removed. Coincidence?

Lipsey, in evidence to the Select Committee on Environment, Food and Rural Affairs, said that the BGRB has "recognised and embraced the importance of greater transparency."[12-2] The body's successor - the GBGB - is apparently "committed" to being "accountable to those that it licences and the public" but I see no evidence of that.[12-19] If anything, I see an industry moving in the opposite direction though from a position where, even many years ago, few doors were left unsecured. An official at Yarmouth was even prepared to lie about the fate of dogs injured on the track. Two One Zero, in only his first race, suffered breaks to a foreleg following collision with another dog. Bozman Ruling sustained a spinal injury, and both dogs were carried from the track and put to sleep. When, however, the track's assistant racing manager Marcus Westgate was quizzed on the incidents the caller was given to believe otherwise; the former placed for adoption and the latter back with the trainer after receiving treatment. As I say, desperate times call for desperate measures.

It is the volunteers working for the adoption centres that so often witness the true meaning of the well used expression "treated as valued athletes." Injuries, neglect and ultimatum - take the dog or he/she will have to be destroyed - come with the territory, and while adoption figures are a great promotional tool (particularly when presented in a misleading way) their value is undermined when rescues speak out. Silence is everything. Probably out of frustration more than anything, Sarah Horner - then Chair of Lancashire RGT (now Lancashire and Belle Vue RGT) - bravely delivered a few home truths in a BVOF posting. It made for unpleasant reading (see p. 59) and I rightly picked up on it for a story to highlight the appalling lack of regard given to racing dogs but again soon afterwards it was a posting deleted. Likewise where rescues feel unable to support racing there is pressure to, at the very least, remain neutral on the subject; their position summed up in a response by Jon Trew, representing Greyhound Rescue Wales (GRW), to a request for information from a pupil for her GCSE project:

> GRW does not hold a position on the banning of greyhound racing. Some
> of our members are opposed to greyhound racing, however as an
> organisation we have to work with greyhound trainers and gain their trust,
> so they will pass on dogs to us at the end of their careers. If they think that
> we are trying to close down their business they are unlikely to pass on
> dogs to us and work with us. Therefore officially we are neutral and do not
> campaign as a group against racing.[12-20]

To not publicly oppose racing is an understandable position to maintain but rescues should never feel they are unable to speak out on issues of welfare. I remember when privately-expressed views by Tracey Seymour (then representing Devon and South-West RGT) were made public. While certainly forthright in her opinion about the treatment of dogs kenneled with trainer Eve Blanchard (see p. 57) the reaction of trainer and owner Dave Smith (and the person behind Greyhoundscene) was inexcusable: "I [have] contacted the RGT and pointed out that [these] forum members have contributed substantial sums to the RGT and comments from Ms Seymour could have an affect on people's willingness to further contribute."[12-21] Is that blackmail? The Trust's Executive Director at the time, Ivor Stocker, did speak with Seymour but wouldn't divulge what was said. Smith further added: "We will be better using the services of those homefinders who are pro-racing, I have no objection to them getting donations and will always do what I can via this forum to raise funds for them."[12-22]

It further brings into question how many cruelty cases witnessed are ever brought to the attention of the RSPCA. I think very few, but politics aside, the rescues do a hard job and those rescues with a responsible homing policy do a fantastic job. If swayed by industry spiel, you'll be thinking the overwhelming majority of racing dogs are destined for someone's sofa and the warmth of a nice fire. A 'mere' 500 was the figure given in the early nineties for greyhounds put down each year; a claim the BBC could "find no basis for" in the making of "Cradle to crave," aired in January 1994. The figure, frankly, is farcical but a similar claim was made by the BGRB in The Telegraph some six years later: "We still haven't got the number of homes we would like for retired racing greyhounds and 500 to 1,000 have to be put down each year."[12-23] Best estimates for 2001 tell a different story: 21,600 bred due to the demand generated by British tracks, and 3,400 rescued/retained... but hey! that doesn't look good at all.

Commonly the public are being misled by given solely a comparison of dogs homed against dogs registered to compete within the regulated sector. No mention is made that about 50 percent of greyhounds bred never make the grade or that a significant number of those homed - thought in the region of 30 percent - are non-graders. And even what figures are given can be wildly out. In two articles from 2011 and 2012 the GBGB are reported saying that "just over 7,000" greyhounds are registered annually for racing. In reality the figures were 7,972 and 7,964 respectively. It is easy to see how registration and homing figures can be used to give the impression that few greyhounds are ever killed. The tactic is employed across the board, and in a briefing for the All Party Parliamentary Greyhound Group (APPGG) the industry governing-body concluded by saying: "With such a tremendous increase in re-homing in recent years, the prospect of the sport re-homing all greyhounds on retirement that are suitable for re-homing is no longer a chimera. Indeed, the sport is moving quickly towards this ultimate goal."[12-24] Of course the importance of winning the support of MPs cannot be overstated and I suspect many are hoodwinked.

At the same time the industry will have us believe it's a grim fate for greyhounds if racing diminished. "The biggest danger of closing tracks is if it went underground," remarked former greyhound commentator and race manager Mick Wheble.[12-25] The implication being no regulation and no monitoring of welfare standards but where do they think a 420 metre track can be hidden? Maybe in the attics of private dwellings belonging to former promoters - I jest, greyhounds don't like stairs - or perhaps the barn of that friendly farmer known to a few of the less scrupulous trainers? Scaremongering, however, invariable takes on a more sinister tone where speculation about the future of a track is rife, as was the case at Oxford in summer 2012 and supported in a shameful article by the local media. 'Greyhounds could be destroyed' was the line taken by contributors including trainer Dave Lee who is quoted saying: "Obviously it's devastating. Being a trainer you never want to put a dog down. I don't know what's going to happen to the dogs, they should be looked after."[12-26]

The article had no substance. Yes, the track was doomed (operations ceased in December 2012) but not the greyhounds. Where similar closures have taken place - I am thinking in particular of Walthamstow and Swansea - we find trainers switching tracks or greyhounds switching kennels, and any dogs that needed a home were found a home. Rescues across the country come together and assist where they can though with Oxford the help on any of the independent rescues was looking unnecessary. The subject was raised in a timely meeting of the Greyhound Forum where it was pointed out "there was ample spare kennelling within the greyhound industry, if not [...] RGT branches, to accommodate any surplus greyhounds," and cash earmarked for prize money and integrity at Oxford in the forthcoming year (2013) "could be used as a contingency for any dogs requiring homes."[12-27] Indeed the irony is, where tracks are facing imminent closure the prospect for many of the dogs is likely more promising than if it was to remain open. Threats made - implied or otherwise - are nothing more than an emotive tool in a last ditch attempt to hang on to their precious track. But again, desperate times call for desperate measures.

It is in stark contrast to the reported increased emphasis being placed on welfare that is receiving lashings of credibility with the apparent healthy working dialogue now enjoyed with high profile and largely respected animal charities under the umbrella of the Greyhound Forum. Meetings are held biannually and groups represented include the GBGB, RCPA, SGV, RGT, RSPCA, Blue Cross, Greyhound Rescue West of England, Battersea Dogs Home, Wood Green and Dogs Trust (their CEO Clarissa

Baldwin chairing discussions). The Forum was born out of a momentous and heated meeting between the welfarists and industry back in 1994 and made possible through the efforts of Baldwin together with vet Paul de Ville. In the formative years its true commercial value was likely lost on the industry but it is now being milked for all it is worth and is guaranteed mention in all self-glorifying publications. I cannot say whether any of the participating charities endorse greyhound racing but it would appear that way regarding the RSPCA, Blue Cross and Dogs Trust as the logos for all three are now proudly displayed on the GBGB website. In PR terms one cannot put a value on that.

Please don't get me wrong, I support the charities engagement with the industry if any gains in terms of welfare outweigh potential benefits pursuing alternative strategies that may result in the industry terminating dialogue. That, however, is a big 'if'. The GBGB is happy talking with what they call "responsible" charities; charities not seeking to change the fundamental nature of greyhound racing in Britain (necessary if the root causes of key welfare issues are to be resolved). What, it must be asked, in terms of welfare has the Forum achieved? I put that question to the RSPCA who felt unable to list one single measure. Baldwin is quoted saying: "There were many times, in the early years of the Forum, when I wanted to throw in the towel. Many a time we attended meetings and were given platitudes or morsels of information to go away with which were designed to keep us quiet until the next time."[12-27] Though according to Baldwin there are achievements: specifically the reformation of the SGV, changes to Rule 18 (covering the responsibility of owners and sadly still failing the greyhounds) and the industry's sign-up to a *voluntary* Charter and Code of Practice, described by Baldwin as "a cradle to grave manifesto" for the greyhounds. Launched in May 2002 it was, in the view of Wood Green, "a strong and tangible indication of the changes which are expected."[12-28] In the view of the BGRB, the industry's own rules were more stringent.

I am hoping there have been *real* benefits for the greyhounds but consideration must also be given to the implications of a greyhound racing industry benefiting from the tacit approval of the likes of the RSPCA. The basis of much discussion in more recent meetings relates to the standard of trainers' kennels, the homing of greyhounds and publication of injury data. On the latter point the Forum could prove very useful to the industry, as outlined in a meeting of the Greyhound Welfare Working Group in 2006: "DL [David Lipsey] suggested that a central characteristic of any industry self-regulation must be that it is open and auditable. He suggested that the group explore whether it would be possible to use the Greyhound Forum as an external group to which the NGRC reported on its activities to provide openness and auditability."[12-29] In other words the Forum could be used as a vehicle to negate ever-increasing calls for public accountability.

It brings us back to the sensitive issue of injuries sustained on the track. I used to think that yearly data relating to injuries would eventually be made public but never raw data and nothing meaningful. I question now the likelihood of publication of figures in any form. It was reported in January 2013 that potentially detailed information on injuries may soon be made available to the Forum but, according to Kinsley promoter John Curran, "strictly under the terms of a confidentiality agreement."[12-30] Under this agreement how can the Forum be considered "an external group"? This is public accountability greyhound racing style and be sure it will be given a positive spin in PR material.

Unnatural bedfellows serving the industry well might best sum up the Forum but there is another charity that, while not a member of the Forum, is certainly useful having 'on side'. I refer to the League Against Cruel Sports (LACS). If there was ever a charity opposing the racing of greyhounds it would surely be LACS, but not so, and the position adopted by the group is given mention under "Welfare: FAQs" on the GBGB website. Lipsey has stated having a "healthy working relationship" with the League.[12-31] Millionaire businessman and greyhound owner Bob Morton, in defending ambitious plans to re-introduce dog racing to Walthamstow, was reported saying "he has been working with the League Against Cruel Sports and the Dogs Trust on his bid."[12-32] Both groups subsequently downplayed their involvement; apparently there was nothing more than an agreement in principle to advise on welfare provisions. I question what input either group could offer on that score but doing so is of course missing the point.

How all this, it is hoped, plays out in reality is perfectly illustrated in an e-mail from of all places Wolverhampton City Council (responding to a brief summary of key welfare issues inherent in greyhound racing and put to the council as it was planning to hold a fund-raising evening at their local track (Monmore)):

> May I say from the outset that the Mayor has looked into the way Monmore Green stadium treats greyhounds and is confident that the stadium views greyhound welfare as a top priority. [...]. It is the Mayor's understanding that the League Against Cruel Sports has acknowledged and accepted that there is no reason to oppose greyhound racing. It is a member, alongside other leading animal welfare charities (RSPCA, Blue Cross, Dogs Trust, Battersea Dogs Home), of the Greyhound Forum which advises the sport's governing bodies on improvements to ensure the welfare of greyhounds is not compromised.[12-33]

Okay, so the author hasn't got all her facts right but from the industry's point of view, who cares? It's perception that counts and you could say 'job done'. The image of greyhound racing is further improved where it is associated with the raising of money for good causes, described as "worthwhile" by the Mayor's office. This was recognised by the industry as far back as the forties when track 'rowdies', tote-ticket forgers and dog-dopers were making the headlines. In 1947 the National Greyhound Racing Society (NGRS) appointed a press officer who moved quickly to improve the 'sports' image. Tactics employed included "the involvement of the NGRS in a number of well-publicised charitable projects. The establishment of a Veterinary Educational Trust and a donation of £10,000 to the Printers Pension Corporation got such activities off to a fast start."[12-34]

Nowadays money is being raised for good causes at all major tracks and it's guaranteed wonderful press coverage. A charity race night at Owlerton, Sheffield, generated £2,313 for the marvellous Helen's Trust. "The money raised from the stadium event will be used to pay for nursing support, sitters, carers and help with running the house of those with terminal illnesses," it was reported. How can you possibly argue with that? "We are keen to help local causes wherever possible," was the comment from the track.[12-35] Cash for Kids is a dog purchased by Shawfield stadium in Glasgow and running for a local radio station's own charity the dog was named after. The black male was said to be "proving a great advertisement for racing at Shawfield, as well as raising money for charity." Racing Manager Daniel Rankin added: "The radio station are fantastic for plugging the dog just before their football coverage. It has all worked out better than we dared hope."[12-36] Win-win partnerships… except for the dogs. I could ask whether it is right that animals are exploited and abused for "worthwhile" causes, but where money is being raised by people outside the industry the issue is perhaps more one of ignorance than morality. The Mayor's office were certainly under the illusion the industry had got their house, or should I say their kennels, in order.

The industry is boxing clever, it needs to, but defending the indefensible is no easy task and there are members of the racing fraternity who will stoop to any level. Credit to Greyhound Star editor Floyd Amphlett for stating: "Debate is healthy but there is no excuse for it ever becoming offensive."[12-37] This, however, is the same editor who has described those who oppose greyhound racing as "swampys" and "screaming loonies." He gets personal and adds: "If you saw the same group of herberts outside a departmental store protesting about anything from the fur trade to the extinction of the Patagonian ridge-backed turtle, you would probably be more concerned about the wildlife living on the protestor."[12-38]

The comments are typical of endless attacks made against not only individuals who dare speak out against greyhound racing but also the media who give them air time. The Alan Titchmarsh Show had, as an occasional feature on the programme, dogs of various breeds seeking a home to include on 3 October 2011 a greyhound named Snoopy (racing name Gorrys Goat). His rescuer, Annie Boddey, gave brief mention of the ex-racer's chequered history and neglect, to which Titchmarsh bravely remarked: "This happens an awful lot with greyhounds doesn't it; once their racing days are finished it seems a lot of people don't care for them."[12-39] For that the station received numerous complaints (not all best worded) and the presenter was called an "absolute arsehole."[12-40] "These feckers [sic] are a disgrace and deserve nothing but sh1t [sic]," was another view expressed.[12-41] As someone who has been threatened with violence for merely asking about the welfare of a greyhound such reactions come as no surprise.

Those clever people at the GBGB must be cringing, and not only at what is being said. When members of the racing fraternity meet opposition in real life they are prepared to go much further than simply being offensive. On last taking part in a peaceful awareness gathering outside Yarmouth stadium a banner was ripped from the hands of a woman in the group and smashed in two. The woman was left visibly shaken. That, however, seems rather trivial in comparison with an incident a few years back when at the same track antis were targeted by a sniper firing from the roof of the stadium. Air rifle pellets were later found but luckily nobody was injured. Few would argue with the sentiment expressed in the subsequent press release issued on behalf of the group: "This insane madness perpetrated against a group of people peacefully protesting is a further indication of the mentality of the people involved [in] and employed by the racing industry."[12-42]

That mentality was greatly in evidence in a campaign hell-bent on dog racing returning to Walthamstow and opposing London and Quadrant's plans for much needed homes on the site of the old track. On 8 May 2012 councillors had their say and approved L&Q's plans. It wasn't a done deal but any chance of the track re-opening was hanging by a thread, and death threats were reportedly made against one of the councillors - Asim Mahmood - who voted for the housing estate. Council Chief Executive, Martin Esom, described it as "a direct threat of physical violence against his family."[12-43] A week later a posting on the Save Our Stow website read as follows: "Saveourstow does not support any threats or violence to anybody... But when you stop democracy and fix voting you ask for trouble."[12-44] Desperate times do indeed call for desperate measures.

I am pleased to say the Save Our Stow campaign failed. It means a few less greyhounds bred, a few less ill-treated, a few less suffering appalling injuries and a few less facing premature death. Looking at the industry as a whole, if it has a future it will be thanks in no small part to the lack of transparency and circulation of, at the very least, misleading information. And working in their favour are the countless and continually changing facts and figures documenting the lives of racing greyhounds. Doubtless many individuals and organisations will seek assurance on welfare from the GBGB website, and due to clever wording and predictable omissions receive that assurance. The GBGB are of course just doing their job but some of what is said lacks any credibility whatsoever. Apparently if greyhound racing was banned it would be fishing next and pet ownership and the entire domestication of animals! Stop laughing at the back.

Anything will be said and done to protect what remains of Britain's greyhound racing industry but in trying to justify its existence, and when all else fails, it comes down to just two words I hear repeated time and time again by grass-roots members and officials alike: "It's legal!" Is that justification for what many greyhounds are subjected to? David Smith using a bolt gun on thousands of greyhounds was apparently legal but it doesn't make it right. And while I would accept that greyhound racing per se is not necessarily illegal there is I believe a strong case in challenging current thinking where dogs are pitted against each other on the dangerously configured tracks we have in Britain. Cue more bullshit from the industry.

97

13

The antis

In the House of Commons back in 1994 MP Colin Pickthall raised the subject of greyhound welfare and was to remark:

> If the NGRC and the government in co-operation do not do something about cruelty to greyhounds, Britain will see a sustained campaign against cruelty in sport. That could damage a perfectly legitimate sport, which I would not want to see damaged or become the subject of the attention of, for example, the League Against Cruel Sports.[13-1]

Needless to say little was done to improve welfare and he was right that a sustained campaign against the cruelty inherent in racing did materialise but it was not the League who ever really posed a threat. Indeed, as already mentioned, the industry has been able to use LACS to their advantage.

Real opposition came with the formation of GA in 1997, and up until more recently the landscape surrounding the plight of dogs bred for racing was relatively clear cut. You had essentially GA - the antis seeking the demise of the industry - and animal welfare charities pursuing measured change seemingly in the belief the humane treatment of greyhounds and commercial greyhound racing as operated in Britain are not incompatible. The later groups significantly, not opposing greyhound racing (though I doubt taking any pleasure in its existence) and thus labelled by industry officials as "welfarists" and "responsible." All at the very least share common ground in their concern for the treatment of greyhounds, and the welfarists are still pushing for a little change here and a little change there. It is though a very different landscape today where opposition to greyhound racing prevails. I see a movement no more co-ordinated than the GBGB are caring for the dogs, and many egos each with their own agenda and delivering a minefield of conflicting information.

When the industry made reference to antis it was GA and support for GA's aims and objectives that comments were directed towards. The group represented the opposition to greyhound racing in Britain and was the brainchild of Tony Peters; a vegan and passionate advocate for cruelty-free living. As the campaign gathered momentum, satellite branches targeting local tracks emerged across the country, while north of the border Greyhound Action Scotland was formed (not so effective). The primary strategy was simple: to raise awareness on key welfare issues by way of street stalls, leafleting and demonstrations. Such activities were developed further and attracted greater media coverage through the staging of national events, e.g. Greyhound Derby Day of Action.

Peters' thinking was to educate as many people as possible and there was sound logic in the strategy. I'm not sure how many people opposed the sickening 'sport' of fox hunting but remember polls indicating it was something like 80-plus percent of the population. It wouldn't matter, however, if it was 99 percent. To end the cruel practice required new legislation. The commercial 'sport' of greyhound racing on the other hand would cease if the public withdrew their support. Never attend or bet on greyhound racing was the key message delivered by GA time and time again. "We are engaged in a gradual process of forcing the industry into terminal decline. When there are fewer races, there will [be] fewer greyhounds bred and then there will be fewer killed. It is as simple as that," said Peters in an article that covered the bungled attempt on the part of track groundsman Andrew Gough to kill a greyhound called Rusty.[13-2]

Raced under the name Last Hope the greyhound became a powerful symbol for the movement with the atrocity marked annually in a fixture still held to this day: Remembering Rusty Weekend (coinciding with the date Rusty was found (2 May 2004)). Greyhound Awareness Week (held towards the end of May) and Greyhound Remembrance Weekend (coinciding with the date the first race meeting was staged on British soil (Belle Vue, 24 July 1926)) are now also established fixtures, though not enjoying the support they once had.

Achieving the same objective via a different route was the thinking behind Virtual Virtues; a campaign launched in 2005 with the aim of persuading bookmakers William Hill to cease all involvement in live greyhound racing and to replace it with virtual (computerised) dog racing. It was supported with posters, leaflets, petitions and postcards. Further targeted initiatives included Winning Words - a drive launched in 2007 to hold leafleting sessions outside race meetings - and Winning Words in the Workplace that saw the distribution of information packs to businesses and sports/social clubs within the catchment area of greyhound tracks. The latter responding to the fact many people who spend a 'night at the dogs' do so as part of a work/club organized night out.

More recent campaigns included the Greyhound Carers Compensation Campaign and Show Some Charity to Greyhounds, both launched in 2009. The latter, essentially education based and providing charities with information on the many welfare implications associated with dog racing, in the hope alternative activities are used as a vehicle for fund raising. The former was set up to, in the words of Peters, "expose just how little the racing industry cares about the greyhounds it makes use of." There are many individuals and independent rescues picking up the pieces - taking care of

99

Dead Certs!

Thousands of greyhounds are slaughtered every year.

Boycott greyhound racing!

Has she just lost the race for life?

Tens of thousands of dogs are disposed of by the greyhound racing industry every year.

Many of them suffer horrifically. Most of them are put to death.

Say "No" to Greyhound Racing!
Don't go to it. Don't bet on it.

Support our campaign to end the slaughter!

William KILL

Tied to a lump of concrete and drowned

Every year thousands of greyhounds suffer and die because of William Hill's involvement in the dog racing industry.

Boycott greyhound racing.
Boycott William Hill.

Please sign our petition

YOU BET...

Thousands of greyhounds are disposed of by the greyhound racing industry every year.

Some of them end up like this.

...THEY DIE

GA posters. Synonymous with the campaign were the slogans and placards used, very much of their time and now being replaced with material reflecting a new era for the movement. Images were frequently criticised by members of the racing fraternity for being out of date or not directly related to greyhound racing in Britain but their use was symbolic and, within that context, the criticism was unfounded

greyhounds that otherwise would be put down when of no further use or value to their trainers/owners - and the idea of the campaign was for these carers to submit compensation claims to cover the many costs incurred looking after the animals. Peters reported: "Two rescues have already submitted claims which the GBGB, disgracefully, has refused to pay."[13-3] It was in short further ammunition for GA.

At its height GA was a force to be reckoned with. The group's website, set up in 2002 and incorporating an international arm, would eventually receive annual 'hits' totalling six figures and helped win support on a global scale. Almost 100 supporters made (in person) their views on the treatment of greyhounds very clear to those attending the racing industry awards' ceremony hosted by the BGRB in 2007, and demonstrations and leafleting sessions were covering 17 of Britain's major tracks. It made possible sustained and co-ordinated objections to any plans for a new track, breeding establishment or trainers' kennels. Where greyhounds made headlines the media were guaranteed letters supporting positive coverage and opposing negative coverage, and any company seen promoting 'a night at the dogs' would receive a barrage of complaints... and yes, it was effective. Battles were won. Winning the war, however, was another matter entirely though it must be pointed out this was a cause supported only by volunteers giving up both time and money. GA had 'right' on its side but lacked resources and I guess what Peters never reckoned on was opposition from within that would ultimately lead to a split in the movement with the emergence of Greyt Exploitations (GE), founded by Trudy Baker, and a movement now fragmented.

Baker's involvement in the campaign and initial support for GA goes back to when the case against David Smith, exposed in The Sunday Times for killing thousands of greyhounds, was being heard at Durham Magistrates' Court early in 2007 (see p. 72). At some time not very long afterwards we got talking and, over a period of a year or so, had numerous conversations and I cannot recall one in which Baker ever spoke positively about the leadership of the movement. In fact it was something Baker questioned, and much of her time was spent putting together a new website while seemingly learning anything and everything she could about the racing industry. It would seem we had a new 'group', not working locally on the ground but rather representing the movement, and people actively involved in the cause were soon receiving e-mail 'action alerts' from GE, in addition to those circulated by GA.

At the time it didn't make a lot of sense. Peters later informed me that Baker had been told her involvement locally with GA activists (in this case based in the North East) was no longer wanted. Knowing Baker as I do, she would have likely experienced meltdown though I believe the long term outcome would be no different. Baker never struck me as the kind of person capable of playing second fiddle to anyone, or even for that matter, being on equal terms. Anyway, the more groups representing the cause the better or so you might think. In Britain we have the likes of Animal Aid and Viva, both very distinctive in their own right and providing a voice for animals on the same (as well as different) issues and doing brilliant work. Baker was perhaps just what the fight against greyhound abuse needed... new energy, new ideas and a new image to a cause admittedly in need of a makeover. If only. I was told Baker had created division in the North East and I have lost count of the many, many reports since of upset and division following in her wake.[13-4]

Differences of opinion are of course inevitable and that applies within any shared area of interest, not least within the 'sport' of greyhound racing, but this person I found extraordinary. I remember one of the first conversations I had with her. Will you please call a certain trainer to find out what has happened to their dog, she asked. The answer was an emphatic 'no' - there was simply no good reason for making the call - but the woman wouldn't drop it and to preserve peace you eventually find yourself giving in. Norfolk-based AFG were 'advised' by Baker not to run with a new leaflet the group had compiled because she didn't agree with all its content. Nor did she agree with a forum posting I had made - not personal but not suiting her agenda - and so an e-mail followed ordering me to remove it. I could go on. She once remarked: "I am in this campaign for the dogs and not to make friends or satisfy some self-serving need - at the end of the day I will compromise but only if those sacrifices ultimately benefit the campaign and of course the dogs."[13-5] On either score I fear Baker has done more harm than good, though never intentionally.

Baker's chief failing is simply a lack of diplomacy but GE did win support through having an okay website when the only competition so to speak was GA's website. Further, Baker gained authority through demonstrating a good knowledge on racings' operations (the importance of both, to establish herself as key figure in the campaign, I'm sure not lost on Baker). Gradually, a notable split in the movement emerged but is GE's strategy and objective any different to GA's?

The first thing to say is GE is running what amounts to little more than a virtual campaign, indeed the 'group' doesn't even have a postal address, not their own that is. Heading the website home page are the words: "Campaigning for the abolition of betting on greyhounds." Though where, it doesn't say. I am assuming Britain, then again it might be a campaign targeting the betting on dogs worldwide. In reality GE does not focus its efforts in this area and greater clarity is given in a brief summary of aims:

> Greyt Exploitations is a non-profit making organisation formed in 2007 and run entirely by volunteers. We strive to raise the public's awareness of the cruel and inhumane treatment of greyhounds and much of our research and investigation work has been published in the national press. This has helped us to effectively campaign for the full enforcement of existing legislation, stronger protection laws and for the gambling on dogs to be outlawed.[13-6]

The reader is still left guessing where but read further and the focus for *much* of the material circulated is Britain, and, as with GA, it is in raising awareness on key welfare issues the 'group' concentrates its efforts. Baker, however, gets side-tracked on matters that frankly are best forgotten. One posting concludes: "Please e-mail the BBC and complain regarding their promotion of a gambling industry as a sport and their endorsement of an industry that depends on cruel practices for its profitability."[13-7] You might wonder if the BBC had signed a new deal to televise greyhound racing but this was in fact in response to Drumcove Lad appearing on A Question of Sport. A great promotional opportunity as already mentioned, but it should be kept in perspective. The BBC were further guilty of, according Baker, "accentuating" greyhound racing when in an episode of EastEnders two characters discuss a visit to "the dogs." It gets worse: apparently the gambling on dogs was referred to as a "bit of a flutter." The value of flagging up the likes of the above is questionable to say the least. Equally, how does it reflect on the movement as a whole?

There is a danger of losing site of the real issues as can be demonstrated in the never ending saga concerning Three Men Go to Ireland, broadcast on BBC2 in January 2010. Dara O'Briain, Rory McGrath and Griff Rhys Jones take a journey through Ireland by way of the canals and rivers, and accompanied by Snip Nua, a greyhound part owned by O'Briain and filmed contending a race at Mullingar. After the programme went out on air it was discovered that 18 days prior to the broadcast the dog had sustained an injury at Harold's Cross, Dublin, and was put to sleep (see p. 51). This was rightly seized upon by the antis. A video of the race perfectly illustrates how the inevitable interaction between dogs competing on oval tracks can lead to serious injury. The case further highlighted the destruction of racing dogs for non life-threatening injuries (Nua had sustained a broken hock - perhaps career-ending but not fatal). And the fact the dog had featured recently in a popular BBC programme and was part owned by a well known comedian could be exploited to gain publicity. I see nothing wrong in that and the story was covered by the Irish Mail on Sunday (31 January 2010) but the focus for Baker and the antis was the BBC for daring to broadcast a programme that included a few minutes of filming at Mullingar - said by Baker to be "a shameful piece of pro-racing propaganda" - and for simply not acknowledging what had later happened to Nua. Almost three months on from when the programme was aired Baker writes:

> The BBC have now admitted to Greyt Exploitations, they were aware of Snip Nua's destruction before the programme was broadcast but have failed to provide us with a reason why they chose not to acknowledge her death, by way of an announcement prior to or at the end of the programme. Or why, at the very least, they failed to inform complainants the BBC were aware of Snip's destruction prior to the programme being aired.[13-8]

To follow we had demonstrations taking place outside venues where O'Briain was performing as part of a UK tour and in March 2012 a petition (not instigated by Baker) was opened calling on the BBC to "please acknowledge what happened to Snip Nua." It had collected 1,604 signatures at the time of writing. For God's sake, drop it everyone! Not a chance, in April 2013 there were plans to take the petition to London to meet a bruised and battered BBC.

Baker was even to take issue with the Corporation over their use of a screen print design of a greyhound for the avatar on a Twitter account without copyright holder Jane Jones' permission. Amusing considering the material Baker has 'lifted' but of course absolutely wrong of the BBC. The matter was rightly taken up by Jones and amicably resolved but quite where it falls in raising "awareness of the cruel and inhumane treatment of greyhounds" I do not know.

People come and go and new 'groups' form as quickly as you can think of a name and register with Facebook, but we had in 2010 one person with aspirations that, if nothing else, highlighted a movement rapidly fragmenting. Christina Hespe had the vision of a "broad, unified, publicly visible campaign" and a first aid kit called the Greyhound Protection Coalition to address what she described as "'cells' operating independently but communicating as and when it is felt necessary."[13-9] I would go further and say there was a climate of secrecy, control and sniping. When the idea of a coalition was put to me, my immediate response was it would never work, or at least never if GE was part of the coalition. It remained only an idea. Much was said at the time that would not be appropriate to cover here and that would test the resolve of Peters. Just six months later the termination of GA was announced in a statement strong on diplomacy:

> As part of efforts to streamline the UK greyhound protection movement,
> Greyhound Action ceased operations in May 2011. Tony Peters,
> Greyhound Action's former UK co-ordinator, who is now helping with the
> organisation of several other animal protection campaigns, had this to say
> about the changes: 'Greyhound Action was just one of several greyhound
> protection campaigns in the UK and this situation was leading to some
> confusion and a considerable duplication of effort. Therefore, in the
> interests of efficiency and effectiveness, a decision was made that
> Greyhound Action should cease operations and encourage its sympathisers
> to support those other campaigns. I continue to be involved in
> campaigning for greyhound protection, but the changes have given me the
> welcome opportunity to spend more time promoting veganism and efforts
> to protect all animals from exploitation and persecution.'[13-10]

There was a degree of continuity maintained with the baton passed on to AFG and marked with the production of a new track leaflet (see following pages) but it was now a much scaled-back operation. A testament, if it was ever needed, to the dedication and hard work of Peters who for many years covered all manner of tasks including press releases, newsletters and campaign material, and whom would think nothing of travelling umpteen miles to give support and solidarity to events being staged across the country. If anything, Peters was doing too much, he was in a sense a victim of his own success, and here for me lies a key problem in developing an effective opposition to greyhound racing in the years to come. Hespe was to write: "I strongly believe that if the various factions of the anti-racing campaign do not get together, form a strategy, work cohesively and politicise this issue, in spite of all the hard work they put in as individuals, they will continue to have a limited effect on the racing industry."[13-11] Who would argue with that? Not me, but a coalition of groups is not an ideal solution, assuming it could ever work in the first place. We have 'groups' breeding like rabbits and it's a dire shame the individuals behind these 'groups' cannot come together and form a team, carrying out different roles and representing the movement in one group (using as a model say, Animal Aid). Perhaps, without

Above/following page: AFG "Running for their lives" track leaflet. Design elements including a new logo for AFG were taken from the GA website. The original leaflet (as depicted here) provided a simple but accurate overview of key welfare issues. It has since been modified for certain groups and not for the better

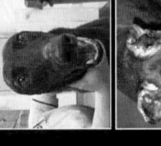

Itchy Scratchy: rescued from kennels at Red Brick Farm, Fengate. Ex-trainer Rebecca Hagger was banned from keeping animals for 10 years for the suffering inflicted on the blue male and another 6 greyhounds.

Dougie: black male found alive with ears cut off in Bedlington, Northumberland.

Little more than enough room to lie down or turn around, no heating or lighting and a floor covered in excrement and urine – conditions that racing dogs have to endure almost every hour of every day.

Hampsey: Irish bred black male found on wasteland near Grimsby dock. It is thought the greyhound would not have survived if found any later.

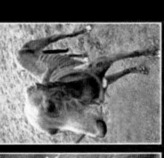
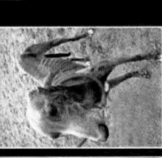

Bleu: thrown over an 8 ft fence onto wasteland in Kirkcaldy, Fife and left to die.

Valentina: heartbreaking case of a heavily pregnant greyhound found brutally killed with both ears cut off in Iron Acton, South Gloucestershire.

Tara: starved nearly to death by Brian Brunton who was banned from keeping animals for life and given an 18 month community order.

"There will always be greyhounds mistreated and abused - that is a fact of life."

Breeder, trainer and owner Richard Newell

paid staff, that will never happen but I am not suggesting people give up anymore time than they already do. It's about making the best use of people's time.

On just the single issue of information published the antis are an easy target for the racing industry. I cannot name one website where information is current and provides clarity and detail on the key welfare issues today, though a proposed much improved AFG website would rectify that situation. Greyhound Safe is one of the better new 'groups' but is taking a broad swipe at the global plight of greyhounds and for how long is questionable. The GA website was in need of a massive overhaul and is now out of date but still 'active' and used by many as a source of information. Is it therefore any wonder we have in the media the reporting of information that is wildly inaccurate, though I do wonder if certain individuals are simply making it up as they go along.

According to the Express, in a report from 2012, up to 40,000 greyhounds are bred every year in Ireland and one team of volunteers saves as many as 200 annually from being burned or buried alive.[13-12] Needless to say no supporting evidence was provided. Two months earlier campaigner Richard Hambleton is quoted by the BBC saying: "There's 25,000 dogs retired each year in racing, on average, across the British Isles. So to replace this they need more dogs but the problem is you breed dogs but you only put one forward out of the litter. That means the rest of the litter is put to sleep."[13-13] I think one word will suffice here: nonsense. In a letter to the Oxford Mail, Susan Smith would have us believe that "most" ex-racers "have their ears cut off and are then left to wander the streets."[13-14] In response GE said: "Excellent letter Susan Smith. Well Done!" It was though rightly condemned by trainers and owners.

When rubbish such as the above is written the antis leave themselves wide open to be discredited by the racing fraternity and how that helps the campaign against greyhound abuse God only knows. Perhaps GE could enlighten us. At the same time, where anything is written in good faith it is difficult to be critical of the authors.

Good faith I am sure is behind the endless petitions, symptomatic of a fragmenting campaign and achieving what? "Ban greyhound racing in the UK." "End commercial greyhound racing in the UK." "Tell the UK Government: ban greyhound racing!" and "Why is it important to stop greyhound racing?" are examples of more recent/current petitions (three current at the time of writing). I know the latter, technically speaking, is merely asking a question but trust me it is anti, it's just not best worded. I've got an idea: why not have one national petition promoted by everyone? That is how it used to be with the GA national petition, now taken over by AFG (the group also managing the William Hill petition).

The profusion of new petitions, many of them track specific and all internet based, reflect both the ease in which petitions can now be set up and the move towards what has been negatively described as "armchair campaigning." The internet though is a valuable tool if used intelligently and has of course the potential to reach a much wider audience than is otherwise possible, particularly through social networking sites such as Facebook. We have in particular GE and Shut Down Belle Vue (SDBV) embracing Facebook, and I would like to say always to good effect. It is, however, where personal differences have been vividly exposed and where a myriad of subjects are covered, frequently off topic and occasionally damaging. GE felt it necessary to post a group photograph of young women at Belle Vue who looked, shall we say, in party mood, and added the title: "A night at Belle Vue 'dog' track." Comments included: "The wrong 'dogs' were racing that night!" and "The only way you could get this lot to run would be to drive by in an ice cream van!" (both comments 'liked' by GE).[13-15] Perhaps GE can again explain how this helps the campaign against greyhound abuse, though it has to be said the above seems positively mild compared with the venom I have on occasion seen directed towards pro-racing views expressed on the SDBV Facebook domain. It is stooping to the level I have come to expect from members of the racing fraternity and will do nothing to win support and change public opinion.

On such an emotive subject, remaining civil and respectful at all times is perhaps asking a lot, but what I shall never understand is the long prevailing animosity across the movement towards the RGT, extending in some quarters to nothing short of loathing, and surfacing in a number of ways. I remember news of a slanging match over the perimeter fence between antis and RGT representatives during one track demonstration (to the shame of *both* groups) but what sticks in my mind is the refusal by a key figure behind a group (anti) I have had a long association with to circulate an appeal made by an RGT branch. To be more specific the appeal came from Friends of Kama's Cave Forum and was for money to help with expensive surgery required to correct a lurcher's hideously deformed front legs (note lurcher: this dog did not fall under the remit of the RGT and was not even being cared for by Kama's Cave; the branch simply wanted to help with a donation). For no other reason, however, than the RGT connection was the appeal rebuffed. I have over the years had a number of discussions with antis on their stance towards the RGT and never once could they justify their position. GA said of the RGT:

> A greyhound rescue set up by the racing industry in the 1970s, largely for propaganda purposes, due to public concern about the fate of ex-racing greyhounds. The launch of the RGT was the equivalent of a tobacco company setting up a hospice for lung cancer victims and many involved in the Trust, especially at a higher level, are fervent supporters of commercial greyhound racing [...]. The industry even goes as far as holding race nights to raise funds for the RGT and there have been occasions where dogs have been seriously injured and even put to sleep at these events. Up until recent years, the RGT only succeeded in finding homes for a few hundred greyhounds annually, but this figure has now gone up considerably, due to increased public awareness of the plight of greyhounds, brought about mainly through the efforts of anti-racing groups, such as Greyhound Action.[13-16]

At the same time, and perhaps surprisingly in light of the above, GA did (to their credit) provide a link to RGT branches on the group website. The antis would do well to remember the RGT are not the enemy. I will make just the following points: the more dogs homed (assuming it is carried out responsibly) is to be welcomed regardless of motive. Indeed the industry (regardless of motive) should be covering homing costs for all greyhounds not retained and that can be homed. You could argue the industry has a moral obligation to cover not only homing costs but further costs following adoption and relating to (say) past injuries incurred on the track. Why should the public (by way of the independent rescues and contributions to the RGT) bail them out (as they do big time)? The short answer is of course, if they didn't many more dogs would be destroyed and that is what the public, the antis and the racing industry should find unacceptable.[13-17]

I sometimes think, give the antis enough rope and they'll surely hang themselves but credit must also be given to the dedication of many grass-roots supporters and, in particular, those raising awareness face to face and holding track demonstrations. You are unlikely to find anyone demonstrating in GE's neck of the woods but SDBV are outside Belle Vue every Saturday, rain or shine, in good numbers. I wouldn't by choice have a debate with them but there is I believe still much value in holding such action. Similar events, in smaller numbers and staged less frequently, can be found at a further 11 or so other tracks in what is a new era for the movement without GA and which is not entirely a bad thing. GA was born out of a strong animal rights' ethos that was very evident in the text and imagery once universally employed, and that is today likely to alienate the cause. A successful campaign must nowadays be more 'presentation aware' and AFG have taken that on board, not least in their new leaflets and track posters.

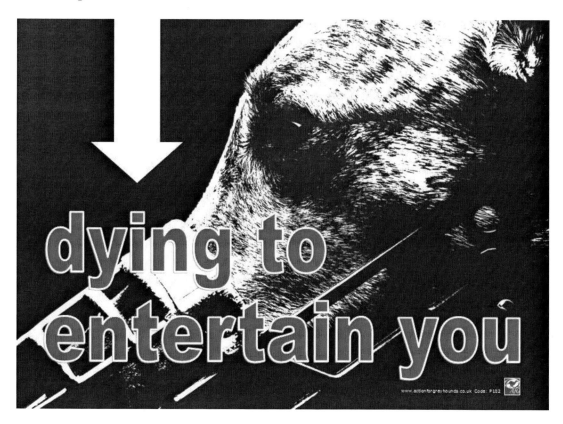

One of the latest AFG track posters delivering a simple but visual strong message

Founded in 1999, AFG is now one of the longest serving groups and, having worked closely with GA, was the natural successor following their demise. On a local level, founding member Annie Boddey, works tirelessly for the greyhounds and is an inspiration to all who know her. If not helping with the rehabilitation and homing of greyhounds discarded by the racing industry, Boddey can be found setting up the group stall at various locations or working on yet more ideas to raise the profile of the cause and invariably covered by the local media. On AFG's ultimate goal to see the welfare of greyhounds protected the group of course has no magic wand but importantly recognises the need (within the movement) for change, first in presentation - on every level - and secondly in strategy.

Many understand only the word 'ban' (it would be a brave soul to suggest anything other than a ban to the likes of SDBV) when essentially it was an end to *commercial* greyhound racing - the racing *industry* - that GA sought, and the difference in terms of winning support with those who can effect change is significant. AFG likewise are calling for an end to *commercial* racing and thus support proposals outlawing the betting on dog racing in the UK, as was drafted in the Racing Dog Protection Act 2009.[13-18] On political strategy, however, AFG believe the focus in the immediate term should be the dangerous configuration of UK tracks and new legislation that would permit only the racing of dogs on a straight course. A milestone in better protection for greyhounds addresses precisely this issue in new policy drafted by the Green Party and supported by AFG.[13-19]

I feel though any progress in politicising this issue is dependent on better representation and this may come from GREY2K USA; a greyhound protection group with proven nous and wherewithal essential in making political headway.[13-20] Rightly in my opinion, much of the focus for GREY2K in America has been the appalling scale of injuries that are inevitable on oval tracks. In September 2012, GREY2K embarked on a fact-finding trip of the British greyhound racing industry and met with LACS and the RSPCA. The former have since been working on a report in conjunction with GREY2K to help determine policy, and while it was all smiles for the camera with Head of RSPCA International, Paul Littlefair, I understand this meeting did not go as well. A request to meet with the GBGB was turned down.

Having the welfarists on side would sure make life easier though I suspect (certainly with the RSPCA) there is as much chance of that happening as there is unity being restored across the movement in Britain. The fall in support on the ground is, I hope, nothing more than activists swapping the banner for the computer. Progress admittedly is painfully slow but the need for fundamental reform is as valid today as it always was.

Top: AFG and supporters on a march through Yarmouth as part of Greyhound Remembrance Weekend 2007. Below: AFG kept very busy flying the flag for greyhounds at Suffolk Dog Day 2011

14

The welfarists

I've never quite 'got' the welfarists. Whilst it is naïve of the extremist-end of the antis to think a ban on anything remotely constituting greyhound racing is ever a realistic possibility (and would be difficult to justify), it is equally naïve on the part of welfarists to think widespread welfare issues inherent in greyhound racing are not insurmountable without addressing the fundamental nature of the 'sport'... as seemingly they do, or at least publicly. Is it though in reality a fear that calling for radical reform (e.g. racing to be conducted only on straight course) might see their seat on the Greyhound Forum withdrawn? Not all sit on the Forum so that might only in part be true. Is it political? Is it simply ignorance? A rumour was once doing the rounds that Annette Crosbie (of welfarists Greyhounds UK) was advised against taking a more radical stance as it may prove damaging for her acting career. I must stress this was only ever a rumour. Does it even matter, you may ask. Well, yes it does, as the welfarists incorporate a number of high profile and *largely* respected groups in a position to effect change. Push them on thinking, however, and you are unlikely to get far (as I have found).

Detail on policy held by all I am not qualified to cover, I question anyway the necessity to do so, and there is much common ground shared by all not least in the minimum standards laid down in the Charter for the Racing Greyhound - the agreed product of the Greyhound Forum and platform for new statutory measures.[14-1] Mention for the purpose of this exercise will be given to four prominent groups in the debate on greyhound welfare and that, in their principal roles, differ greatly: the Dogs Trust, LACS, RSPCA and Greyhounds UK. The above came together in a series of meetings to identify common ground on proposals for new legislation and on which much rested for the welfarists, first in the Animal Welfare Act 2006, and secondly in new measures made under Section 13 of the Act that would address specifically better protection for racing dogs, namely the Welfare of Racing Greyhounds Regulations 2010. It was to be the culmination of 15 years of talks and promises and ultimately proved, for all but the racing industry, a massive disappointment due to its limited scope. Confined in the main to trackside activity, the Dogs Trust branded it a "whitewash."

Essentially, the new legislation would provide minimum welfare standards across all tracks in England and largely bring the independent tracks in line with those tracks licensed under the GBGB. Key detail included the requirement for a vet to be present at all race/trial meetings and greyhounds to be examined by a vet prior to racing/trials (and withdrawn if judged not fit to run), the provision of suitable veterinary facilities and kennels to accommodate as a minimum 20 percent of dogs attending, the identification of greyhounds raced/trialled by way of both earmark and microchip and the recording of injuries sustained.

Its limited scope to one side, the welfarists broadly accepted the proposed minimum *track* standards as presented in a public consultation held by DEFRA (30 April 2009-22 July 2009). Concerns were expressed and amendments made (I believe 18 in total) to appease in part both sides and covering a variety of areas (e.g. veterinarian related measures to encompass sales' trials and the date to be included when recording injuries) but notably track configuration - the root cause of the majority of injuries - was never mentioned. Welfarists rightly, however, used the consultation process to highlight their broader concerns. The Dogs Trust stipulated a need for statutory minimum welfare standards to apply across tracks, breeders, trainers and owners premises, and added: "It is essential that welfare standards apply throughout the dogs racing careers and to everyone dealing with racing dogs."[14-2] The Trust further called for a single, centralised database holding relevant details of *all* dogs (regardless of where raced) from the time of stud book entry into retirement.

At the time the Trust was to reiterate their belief that self-regulation had not worked and that "without statutory regulation the welfare of the greyhounds will always be compromised because of financial priorities."[14-3] The following year, however, there was a shift in opinion with it now apparently judged "the best way forward" by Chief Executive Clarissa Baldwin and "colleagues."[14-4] A further year on and Baldwin states in a letter dated September 2011 and published in the Greyhound Star: "The 'industry' is certainly a very different organisation to that which we had to deal with five to ten years ago. There has been huge progress (still a little way to go!) but credit where it is due and there is little doubt that 'welfare' is now recognised."[14-5] Still a *little* way to go? As previously detailed, research indicates no more than about half the dogs bred to meet British demand will be rescued/retained (and what life for those retained?) and the number of injuries sustained annually is a five figure sum!

And the Trust talks about "cradle to grave" welfare seemingly in the belief this is something that can be achieved within the commercial environment. When Bob Morton cleverly 'teamed up' with both the Trust and LACS in his doomed proposal to bring greyhound racing back to Walthamstow, Baldwin was quick to clarify the charity's position: "Were planning permission to be granted, our priority would be to ensure the cradle to grave health and welfare of the dogs who train or race at the track."[14-6] Really? This would be greyhound racing on an oval-like configured track that cannot be made safe. I knew that, *perhaps* the Trust knew that, but if they're going to imply otherwise where is the supporting evidence? This I requested in a series of e-mails and of course it was not provided. Admittedly I was being a little mischievous, but if real progress on greyhound welfare is ever to be made it's important the welfarists recognise and acknowledge the relevance of track configuration to the high levels of injury as seen Britain.

Supporting evidence I sought also from LACS when, in an e-mail, the charity was to state: "We disagree that an oval greyhound track can never be made safe for the dogs participating."[14-7] A request was made several times for the evidence before I was even afforded the courtesy of a response. Eventually, more than two months later, LACS at least acknowledged no such evidence existed and there was seemingly a minor shift in position: "We don't have evidence, and hence we say that we *believe* oval tracks to be *safer* [emphasis added]. We have met with the GBGB and urged them to invest money into research on this issue. True to form, they have gone quiet on the issue."[14-8]

LACS is surely the one group you would expect to be spearheading a campaign against the suffering inflicted on dogs bred for racing - the clue is in the name (greyhound racing being as much of a 'sport' as say fox hunting) - but on the charity website just four short pages (and a mere 760 words combined) are given exclusively to their greyhound racing campaign, plus the very occasional blog (the last referencing the meeting that took place with GREY2K USA) (correct on 28 June 2013). The group though, to their credit, have produced a strong-on-design leaflet supporting the campaign. It looks professional but is sadly weak on content, providing (like the website) vague, inaccurate and out-of-date information (e.g. "part of the surplus [annually] is 2,500 UK bred young dogs who fail to make the grade as racers").[14-9] It is perhaps worth noting, such material is compiled by paid staff with (I would have thought) more resources at their disposal than any anti.

The League, established in 1924, campaigned for decades for a ban on hunting wild mammals with dogs and when (in the early noughties) a ban was in sight it was time, in their words, "for the League to tackle the problems present in other cruel sports, greyhound racing being one of these."[14-10] A new campaign to improve the lives of greyhounds was launched in June 2003 but I have always felt the League - or should I say its board of trustees - has failed to grasp any true understanding of the 'sport', more so than other welfarists. Injuries to one side, the League rightly identifies profit as driving business and, as such, "the dogs are generally seen as animal business commodities."[14-11] This of course will always be reflected in their care and disposal but the League then states: "Don't give your money to the greyhound industry before it cleans up its act."[14-12] Let's hope something positive comes out of the work carried out in conjunction with GREY2K.

What is their position as I write? This being difficult to ascertain from the internet, I had a LACS representative clarify matters. Primary concerns (as detailed in an e-mail, 12 March 2013) cover over-breeding and the lack of recorded data on dogs bred for racing, the fate of non-graders (Irish bred in particular) and ex-racers, social deprivation and physical stress/injuries suffered. The League is apparently calling for 1) the Animal Welfare Act 2006 "to be used to set standards to protect dogs from the cruelty they currently face," 2) a single regulatory authority and 3) a compulsory levy from bookmakers assigned specifically for welfare. Figures sent match those on the internet/in the leaflet and are inaccurate. No figure for the above levy was given but in an e-mail dated 2 August 2011 the League stated "about" three percent.

Listed as a Vice President of LACS is Annette Crosbie; the founding member of Greyhounds UK that (as does LACS) enjoys endorsement from a number of celebrities. Crosbie, however, more so than any other individual has put the subject of greyhound welfare on the map. The thinking behind Greyhounds UK was, according to Crosbie, to achieve publicity, and to this end her status as one of Britain's best-loved actresses has been used to good effect, though not to the delight of all her fans. It was reported in the Mail that a £16-a-head audience with the actress were "subjected to a rant on the plight of greyhounds" with many storming out during an interval. The response from Crosbie was typically resolute: "In the future I will compare my 53 years in the entertainment business to greyhounds whose racing career is just 18 months. I think that will work."[14-13]

And with the exception of antis, no one is more outspoken on greyhound welfare and the racing industry where, in the words of Crosbie, there is "no transparency, no accountability and a code of, if not secrecy, certainly cover-up." The priority is "a guaranteed, constant supply of dogs on the race card for the bookmakers," and "when a dog leaves the NGRC tracks it leaves the NGRC consciousness." But (as with all welfarists) Crosbie is not seeking an end to the industry she so vehemently attacks. "The issue is not whether greyhound racing should be banned but why successive governments, over 75 years, have turned a blind eye to the way this self-regulating gambling industry operates."[14-14]

That said, and while in the past Crosbie has focused on better protection for dogs where a new track is proposed, the actress gave support in person to an anti-rally being staged outside the old Walthamstow track in June 2012 (when the future of the derelict site had yet to be secured). Perhaps Crosbie and Greyhounds UK sit somewhere on the periphery. While supportive of the Charter, Crosbie also described it as a "rudimentary book of rules which are not binding on anyone, even those who bother to read it."[14-14]

In the group submission as part of the consultation on new regulations for racing dogs there was again a call for trainers and breeding establishments to be included in new minimum standards and a broader greyhound data base to encompass details from the time of stud book entry into retirement (and to capture all dogs entered in the "UK Stud Book" (whatever that is)). Greyhounds UK of course had issue with the subsequent limited movement on the part of DEFRA, as did all welfarists, but in a surprise move a long-time representative of the group, Maureen Purvis, submitted a petition calling for the Prime Minister to withdraw the proposed regulations. The accompanying text read as follows:

> These regulations cheat greyhounds out of the protection they deserve for
>
> the 99 percent of their time spent in kennels while racing and, when they
>
> are no longer able to race, protection from abandonment or destruction.
>
> They allow greyhounds to continue to be kept away from any independent
>
> publicly accountable inspection, defeating the purpose of the Animal
>
> Welfare Act. The consultation on these regulations dismissed objections
>
> from over 10,000 concerned citizens and animal welfare organizations,

allowing the Greyhound Board of Great Britain unfair influence during the preparation of these regulations which benefit them and allows them to continue to treat the greyhounds as they wish.[14-15]

Crosbie made reference to it in a blog that offered an insight into the democratic process:

> We have got a petition on the number 10 website for greyhounds. Never let it be said that we left the dogs to the mercy of a gambling business because we were told to by a member of the House of Lords who was acting as a consultant for that business. The way he put it was profit comes before welfare. Any regulations about welfare were 'aspirational'. So, if any of you want to join us in poking a stick into this so-called democratic process, here is the website address.[14-16]

"Poking a stick" is the best that could be said of it. It would change nothing, and in that sense was pointless. At the time I went further and described it as extraordinarily misguided. The petition would make more sense coming from the financially strapped track operators that within the independent sector would face red tape like never before and a substantial increase in costs to meet the new requirements (perhaps resulting in track closures though DEFRA were keen to avoid this).

On welfare, yes the proposals fell short of naïve expectation on the part of welfarists. Is that, however, reason to scrap them? Better surely, to have limited protection specific to racing dogs than none at all and the new measures contained one vital component: the requirement for a vet to be present throughout meetings and trials (rarely the case at flapping tracks), and vital because of the horrifying scale and nature of injuries suffered by greyhounds on the track. The new measures, if properly enforced, would therefore ensure the immediate treatment of the many injured and possibly prove the best statutory protection given to racing dogs but the petitioner (and more than 1,300 signatories to likely include members of the racing fraternity) wanted them withdrawn. In another bizarre twist the ill-conceived petition got the backing and promotion of GE, or should I say Trudy Baker, though she was coming at it from a different angle and had failed to do her homework.[14-17]

Credit, nevertheless, to Greyhounds UK and Crosbie in particular for giving greyhounds a voice because, as Tony Peters was so acutely aware, it is probably through raising awareness that the greatest change will come. Among welfarists, Crosbie is the maverick. She has described promises on the part of the racing industry to improve welfare as "all lies."[14-18] And it was said by Greyhounds UK that "a culture of institutionalised animal cruelty has developed within the greyhound industry, sanctioned by government."[14-19] Now in her senior years (born 1934, reportedly) I wonder if Crosbie has much fight left in her. The Greyhounds UK website is now down (permanently?) and blogs are noticeable by their absence… but the paradoxes remain. While believing that our relationship with animals should never be based on money why not at least put her name to calls for the end to *commercial* greyhound racing? And no one is more aware of the risk of injury to dogs competing on oval tracks but reference to track configuration is on merely the degree of radius. Crosbie, however, does offer an explanation on there being nothing more than a half-measured approach on the part of some charities:

> I understand that charities have a problem protesting about the treatment of racing greyhounds. Unless the charity is there for greyhounds specifically, its supporters could complain about the concentration on one breed, some of its supporters may be followers of greyhound racing and the Charity Commission may still disapprove of charities getting involved in political campaigning.[14-18]

I'm not sure where LACS stand on the latter but among much controversial media coverage surrounding the RSPCA, the charity more recently was accused of pursuing "what is clearly a politically motivated campaign against a hunt which operates within [Prime Minister] David Cameron's community."[14-20] The comment was reference to the RSPCA launching an unprecedented prosecution for unlawful fox hunting by the Heythrop hunt, and okay it was made by one of the accused, Vanessa Lambert, but the case was ultimately to cost the RSPCA near £327,000. Branded a "politically motivated animal rights' organisation" by the Countryside Alliance - again no surprise there - it was pointed out by the judge that members of the public may feel the money could be more usefully employed.[14-21]

It's not exactly the RSPCA treading safe but where greyhounds are concerned it would seem the charity is taking a very conscious detour to avoid all *licensed* trainers' kennels en route to our courts. Indeed RSPCA preference, they have told me, is that whenever possible the welfare standards should be enforced by the industry. The one prosecution I can think of in more recent years concerned the Freeman's where, following a stipendiary steward inspection, the RSPCA were called in (see p. 70). And yet the RSPCA have recognised that many trainers' kennels are far from adequate to meet standards as laid down under Section 9 of the Animal Welfare Act (see p. 57). Further, as previously mentioned, an estimated 30 to 40 percent of the dogs suffer from fleas and worms - again a breach of the above Act - with the condition of some found to be truly appalling. I'm digressing but if mention is given to the position of the RSPCA on greyhound racing, mention must also be given to their role in the policing of welfare.

Members of the racing fraternity will dispute allegations of neglect and ill-treatment by referencing legislation - chiefly the Animal Welfare Act - that covers the protection of racing dogs as well as other animals wherever kept; a point DEFRA and government are quick to remind us. It is, however, failing the dogs and I find it ironic that the body we look to, to enforce animal welfare law - the RSPCA - were damning of the Welfare of Racing Greyhounds Regulations for not addressing this issue: "The failure to provide regulation for greyhounds whilst at trainers' premises is a considerable missed opportunity."[14-22] My grievance in part with the RSPCA is not who the group choose to prosecute (I congratulate them for taking on the Heythrop hunt) but who they choose not to, and their logo proudly displayed on the GBGB website adds insult to injury. It is though a sad state of affairs where, as is the case in Britain, enforcement of animal welfare law is so frequently dependent on private prosecutions.

While echoing the concerns of many welfarists regarding the new regulations - reiterating in particular the call for one centralised database - the RSPCA further questioned the need for both tattoo markings and a microchip for identification purposes, recognising the former is painful to implement and thus a welfare issue (sadly too often overlooked). Overall, in the view of the charity, the new measures were a "step in the right direction."[14-22] Again though, in common with all welfarists enjoying that view from on top of the fence, when it comes to addressing the root cause of key welfare issues inherent in greyhound racing the RSPCA have little to say.

In a letter dated 30 July 2012, I put a few questions to the charity and chiefly one that must fill any welfarist with dread: In principle, do you have any objection to greyhound racing in its current form? If the answer to the above question is 'yes' but you are not against greyhound racing in any form how would you like to see it conducted? I helped the RSPCA along by defining 'form', this being the key elements that characterise greyhound racing in Britain: a commercial enterprise where up to six greyhounds - primarily acting as a betting medium - compete against each other on all-sand tracks that are oval-like in configuration with a radius of bends up to 50 metres thereabouts. Simples. Answer please.

What I got was their policy on dog racing, word for word, in its entirety as detailed in RSPCA Policies on Animal Welfare - a total of just 147 words! - with a further paragraph added (to save face?) and much of the text was off topic. On specifically the racing of dogs, the following is stated: "The RSPCA is opposed to the racing and training of dogs where distress or injury result from the placing of excessive demands upon the animal."[14-23] That being the case the RSPCA is surely against greyhound racing as operated in Britain? Not so, despite the catastrophic number of injuries suffered by the dogs every year. The RSPCA, in their response to the APGAW and Donoughue reports, concur that surface, design, dimension and maintenance of tracks are "likely to have an impact" on the welfare of greyhounds but reference is never given to the fundamental problem: parallel straights leading into tight bends. And their opinion that "two industry-commissioned research projects into track surface and design should be taken into account when forming guidelines for track standards," is perhaps indicating a failure to understand the cause of so many injuries... or simply a cop-out?[14-24]

The broad agreement among welfarists, however, that a veterinarian must be present at all races and trials, acknowledges the risk of injury. It is where unity across all stakeholders exists bar the flapping community where, for economic reasons, it was generally the norm to not have a vet on site. "There can be no justification in our day and age for this," said then Chairman of the BGRB, David Lipsey.[14-25] It is not simply the need for badly injured greyhounds to receive immediate treatment but, as was noted in a Monopolies and Mergers Commission report as far back as 1986, "without an official veterinary surgeon present unfit greyhounds might be raced."[14-26] The only grey area is on schooling tracks, but there is one body - a counterpart of the RSPCA - who are not convinced. I refer to the Scottish SPCA.

The Welfare of Racing Greyhounds Regulations covers only England, and while the same legislation could be adopted in Scotland on the back of the Animal Health and Welfare (Scotland) Act 2006, there are no plans to do so. The reason given by the governments Animal Welfare Policy Team is the above Act is "sufficient to ensure that the welfare of racing greyhounds is adequately met," and yet it offers no more protection to such dogs than our own Animal Welfare Act.[14-27] We have therefore in Scotland no requirement for a vet to be present at trials and races held within the independent sector. At the time of correspondence with the policy team there were five flapping tracks operating in Scotland, compared with seven in England and two in Wales and thus it was, and remains, an issue very relevant for Scotland.

In 2010, I contacted the Scottish SPCA to ask whether the charity was actively seeking the Scottish Parliament to adopt the same welfare measures given to greyhounds in England and the answer was no. The justification was the minimal complaints the charity had received on flapping tracks. This is the same organisation that some two years earlier is reported saying:

> Some unregulated tracks are better than others. But as an example, we
>
> know of a case where a dog was injured and lay disembowelled on a
>
> flapping track in agony for 40 minutes because no vet was in attendance to
>
> offer immediate euthanasia. When we went to investigate the next day, no
>
> one would give us any information.[14-28]

Of course such communities operate as closed shops but it's no different to the flapping tracks in England. Is the lack of complaints just a convenient excuse? The Scottish SPCA was asked what, in an article I had written outlining the key welfare concerns relating to tracks/racing in Britain, was not relevant to Scotland, to which they replied: "I can appreciate that this information is nationwide."[14-29] Their position, however, did not change. It takes some believing but a representative of the group was even to express support for a new track proposed at Wallyford, East Lothian (at the time of writing partially constructed but with completion uncertain).

As I said at the beginning, I've never quite 'got' the welfarists. Across their ranks there was a gathering of momentum, strength and unequivocal opposition towards IGB plans to export greyhounds to China, and rightly so, but within a properly regulated framework would the quality of life and fate of those dogs be any different to many greyhounds bred to meet British demand? Arguably not. Perhaps the fence the welfarists are sitting on is so high they have lost sight of what is happening on the ground. Perhaps the view enjoyed from up there is preventing a shift in position or perhaps it's all just a bit too close to home. Above anything, there appears to be naïve thinking that problems can be fixed without fundamental change.

The Dogs Trust conveyed a need for the development of a system that matches the number of dogs entering racing with the number that can be re-homed. Firstly I would hope the Trust actually meant the number of dogs bred for racing and secondly, within a commercial environment where costs dictate the animals' future, that will never happen, not least in Ireland where greyhounds as pets remains an alien concept. The RSPCA has called for the training of trainers to reduce the number of non-graders, "with methods based on positive reward systems" (for the dog or for the trainer?).[14-30] Speed of course is everything in greyhound racing and whether employing "positive rewards systems" or not, it is the fastest dogs making the grade. I'm losing the will to live. All four groups (Dogs Trust, LACS, RSPCA and Greyhounds UK) felt that if "prize [and run] money at greyhound races was higher this would also increase the dogs' value to their owners resulting in better treatment."[14-31] Winning the lucrative and prestigious tournaments (e.g. William Hill Greyhound Derby) increases their value, chiefly though as breeding machines and thus a broken hock would never result in euthanasia. For your graded runner any modest increase in race money the industry could afford equals also an increase in losses when out through injury and taking the space of a new dog that is able to earn its keep. Money merely influences their value as commodities and not as sentient beings.

If the welfarists had a mantra it would be this: "Our objection is not to racing, it is to the causing of suffering," said by LACS.[14-10] I could say the same but, unlike the welfarists, recognise fundamental changes are required to end the suffering. The welfarists' position covers all bases and is ultimately flawed as the humane treatment of greyhounds and *commercial* greyhound racing are simply incompatible.

15

Conclusion

Greyhound racing in Britain is not a sport but rather an industry fuelled by and feeding a culture of betting, and dependent on morally repugnant practices for its very survival. Reference is even made to the meat trade in justifying its legitimacy: "Each year tens of thousands of animals are butchered for meat. Birds are shot for sport, wild animals are kept in safari parks and fish swim in aquariums for human amusement," said by editor of Greyhound Star, Floyd Amphlett.[15-1] His point being the public exploit animals or sanction the exploitation of animals and he claims 99.9 percent of the public do not care that greyhounds are exploited for entertainment. Yet this is the same editor who, in common with industry officials, will not publish welfare related information that is deemed too sensitive, and just for the record it is nearer 1,000 million animals killed in the UK every year for food (excluding fish) (the industry was never good on detail, particularly regarding animal welfare).

Amphlett has further declared "that short of another 'Seaham' type episode [...] we are not the naughtiest kids in class."[15-2] When it comes to the leisure industry and animals used in competition, where it is perhaps reasonable to make comparisons (though of course two wrongs never make a right), who then are the "naughtiest kids"? There exists within horse racing many similarities but on a smaller scale and no other competitive activity comes close. In terms of injuries, greyhound racing on oval-like configured tracks has no equal, whether a sport, working or otherwise.

We are told greyhounds, unlike horses, can survive broken legs. I could in response say treatment is expensive and the majority of racing greyhounds have little value but that is of course missing the point. We should be looking at the cause and not the symptom and that is where the Welfare of Racing Greyhounds Regulations 2010 failed in protecting greyhounds at tracks. It isn't natural for an animal to turn 180 degrees at full speed and all tracks would benefit from a bigger circumference - not the view of an anti but the GBGB's own track safety consultant John Haynes. Racings' "obsession with pace and power might be excusable if we had increased the radius of our turns," remarked greyhound veterinarian Paddy Sweeney.[15-3] Do officials though even recognise a problem? It has been suggested that policy of various tracks is to deliberately grade for trouble. Amphlett believed only a "small minority grade for trouble on the misguided premise that 'it is what BAGS would want'."[15-4] Whether given a 'helping hand' or not, interaction between runners - the cause of many of the more serious injuries - cannot be prevented on oval configured tracks and is arguably seen as an intrinsic element of a 'sport' where the greyhound is both chaser and victim.

What, however, I must concede is greyhounds love running and that we are reminded time and time again but what does race day entail? Answer: about 30 seconds (for the standard distance of four bends) risking life and limb, possibly four-plus hours in a track kennel for a typical race meeting and maybe two, four, six hours or sometimes much longer on the road in cages not even big enough to turn around in when transported to and from the meeting. On the 'open' circuit it is perfectly feasible to have say a trainer based in Essex running dogs at Newcastle.

In the name of welfare, ironically, there is much talk about extending racing careers (to reduce breeding figures) and to this end dogs running on flapping tracks following retirement under GBGB rules is viewed positively by all bar the antis, but in the name of welfare dogs should never be subjected to the risks applicable to all tracks in Britain. From a welfare point of view, race day is at best for the greyhound intermission from boredom and I am sure for many, misery, confined for most hours of most days in 'training' kennels of wildly varying standards. "If the public were fully aware of the conditions suffered by racing greyhounds, the Society believes they, like us, would be appalled," said the RSPCA, who we hope have at least mentioned their concern to the Greyhound Forum.[15-5]

Not yet given mention (and thus must included here) is the use of drugs to improve/impair the animal's performance.[15-6] No sampling and testing exists within the independent sector and how widespread the abuse is under the Rules of Racing we cannot be sure as, according the Independent Anti-doping and Medication Control Review, testing across both trials and racing is limited to about one in 60 runners. Nonetheless 202 'positives' were identified for the years 2006-9 and the subject is taken very seriously by racings' governing body, though be under no illusion as to why: "Approximately £2 billion is wagered annually on 'the dogs' in Great Britain and the betting public must be protected."[15-7] In the world of greyhound racing integrity trumps welfare every time.

Integrity further disqualifies any runner for merely looking at another dog in a trial/race, and what soon became apparent in the surveys I carried out is that disqualified dogs would rarely return to racing and very few are subsequently listed on greyhound-data.com either available for adoption or adopted. This I fear is a scandal yet to be uncovered. "Deliberate interference," as it is termed, may single out a dog as not suitable/no longer suitable for competition but is not a definition for aggression. How many though are conveniently put down, with the box "unsuitable as a pet" ticked on the GBGB 'retirement' form?

By the same token we have many greyhounds that retire through injury and are placed for adoption. Okay, the responsibility for any short-term treatment required is frequently given to rescues (left with the owner the animal would likely be destroyed) but a happy ending all the same, or so you might think. Sadly for many ex-racers the rigours of racing linger on and it is a subject that for obvious reasons is rarely given mention but should be. It is covered in part by veterinarian John Kohnke who states:

> A common reason for retirement is either wrist or hock injury, with internal bone or ligament damage. These joints are subjected to high loading stress when galloping and cornering at speed. Often, in older age, the damaged joint surfaces develop cartilage erosion and degenerative joint disease. The damaged joints may also begin to show reduced flexion or in more severe cases, pain and discomfort on flexion or lameness when weight bearing.[15-8]

Other less common reasons given for retirement include "severe muscle wastage due to stress-induced acidosis or hyperthermia, 'racing thirst' and chronic 'cramping'. Many of these greyhounds are retired to a life of ongoing physical disability and recurring medical problems."[15-8] The same vet has a Q and A section in the Greyhound Star in which a reader sought advice for a 12-year-old ex-racer "crying in pain." It was noted in the response: "In your case, the history of a broken hock, especially if it is stiff and less flexible, is probably the major reason for the pain due to arthritis."[15-9] In the Salisbury Journal details of a greyhound in the care of Greyhound Rescue West of England are given:

> Boozer, a four-year-old greyhound, was handed in to GRWE by his trainer when a hock injury forced his retirement and he currently lives at a foster home after attempts to find him a permanent home failed because he was unable to walk far. His condition will not improve so the charity is appealing for a home in south Wiltshire that can offer him love and attention but where he would not be expected to walk for longer than 10 minutes at a time.[15-10]

I can provide personal experiences having adopted greyhounds since the eighties but the point is made. Doubtless there are cases where quality of life must be questioned. Doubtless saving a greyhound's life is not always the humane option. And privately there are likely members of the racing fraternity thinking this is the consequence of interfering do-gooders, antis and welfarists (in the past the animals automatically put down). Again we should be addressing the cause. In addition we have those greyhounds suffering either physically and/or mentally as a result of ill-treatment and greyhounds that are still ending up on the street.

All the while the industry PR machine is working overtime to keep the business of greyhound racing afloat, to keep the bookies happy, to keep the punters happy. "Racing greyhounds are treated as valued athletes," we are given to believe. "The standard of care and personal attention lavished on them probably exceeds the care given to most dogs kept as pets."[15-11] Sounds good and if true why not silence all the critics in one fell swoop with a racing kennel open day? Not one or two carefully chosen kennels but every kennel. The industry wouldn't dare. While having to concede injuries occur, we are given to believe safety has improved significantly but never will raw data be published and never, never, will the GBGB let it be known how many greyhounds (detailed in retirement forms) are put down as a result of injury.[15-12] What the public are given instead is highly misleading information, sometimes simply inaccurate information and a defence that on occasion would not look out of place in an episode of Monty Python's Flying Circus.

In 2013 the cost of greyhound racing is still making the headlines. Norman, as he is now known, is a greyhound that never made the grade to race and was found abandoned in Newtownabbey, Northern Ireland, in June 2013 with both ears hacked off. Just 18 months' young at the time, Norman received all the care you could wish for and is thankfully doing well. In May 2013 another sickening discovery: nine rotting carcasses of greyhounds on farmland in County Wexford (the second find of its kind for farmer Trevor Foxton). And the fate of many adopted greyhounds remains a lottery with trainers/owners eager to get rid of 'redundant stock' as quickly and cheaply as possible. Greyhounds to include Lamars Girl, disqualified for "deliberate interference" in a trial at Sheffield (9 June 2012), given away to God knows whom and in February 2013 found dead in a lay-by a short drive from Owlerton stadium. Greyhounds to include one identified in the media only as being five years old and found severely emaciated by the side of a road in Corby. Conscious but unable to move the poor greyhound could not be saved.

It is though a different industry to that even a decade ago. RGT figures have doubled since the early noughties and in the last few years reports of greyhounds inhumanely killed have dwindled. Dogs in Britain are no longer being shot by 'the local man with a gun' or sent to the abattoir, or at least not that we know of. The GBGB have further gained UKAS accreditation for ensuring standards as laid down under the Welfare of Racing Greyhounds Regulations (and thus tracks operating under the GBGB do not have to be licensed by local authorities) but what this has done in essence is safeguard self-regulation that many will argue is not in the best interest of greyhound welfare. And how many truly believe anything would be different if it wasn't for the bad publicity the industry has received? A milestone was (for sure) the exposure of greyhound executioner David Smith in 2006 (see p. 72). The important question is, are greyhounds viewed any differently? Sadly not is the impression I get from speaking with racings grass-roots' members. Trainers are undoubtedly passionate about greyhound racing but I have yet to speak to a single trainer who conveys the same passion for greyhounds.

The big positive over the last decade is that the number of greyhounds unaccounted for and presumed killed has fallen dramatically, in part due to a rise in greyhounds adopted and thanks chiefly to the fall in dogs bred (26,077 (2003) fuelled by racing in Britain, falling to 15,555 (2012)). Bad publicity has forced the industry to place greater importance on greyhound welfare, but more importantly it has resulted in dwindling support for greyhound racing that in turn has seen a fall in the number of meetings staged and that in turn has seen a fall in the demand for racing dogs. Here credit can be given to the antis (as well as the media though their objective was always to sell newspapers).

"The antis were always more of an irritation than a threat," writes Amphlett, "and that threat eased considerably with the introduction of the Animal Welfare Bill."[15-13] Not true but what I will concede is today (2013) the industry have little to fear from the antis. Trudy Baker is selling greyhound 'racing jackets' that advertise her website while outside Belle Vue on 13 July there was a fracas between protesters, with a member of the group arrested and cautioned. The movement is today lacking representation and co-ordination, the plight of greyhounds is being lost in the competition for most 'likes' on Facebook, and whether any news is circulated or not is decided on origin and not content. Can it be fixed? AFG gives me hope but it is wholly dependent on the *right* people coming together, agreeing policy and working as a team.

Along the way some clever initiatives on the part of Tony Peters and GA have been lost and should be resurrected. I am thinking in particular of Virtual Virtues and Winning Words in the Workplace. In relation to the former it was noted in BGRB evidence to APGAW that "greyhound turnover in betting shops has been weak in the face of competition with 'virtual' greyhound racing and fixed-odds betting terminals."[15-14] More recently The Economist was to report:

> Since 2008 the gross gambling yield (a measure of profit) generated by betting on dogs in bookmakers has fallen by 20 percent to £240 million [...]. Over the same period the profit generated by fixed-odds betting terminals of all kinds has increased by 37 percent to over £1.4 billion - more than the total made from horses, dogs and football combined. Greyhounds are less important to the bookies than ever.[15-15]

This undoubtedly is the way forward for the gambling industry that would make huge savings with the elimination of BAGS fees and the voluntary levy on betting turnover but of course the biggest winners are the greyhounds. Why antis are not pushing this is a mystery. I believe, however, the original campaign would be better remodelled so the virtues of 'virtual' racing are simply promoted and no one bookmaker is targeted (as was originally the case (William Hill)). Resurrecting Winning Words in the Workplace would logistically prove a greater challenge and it highlights the lack of resources - both manpower and money. A result of the movement fragmenting is funding is now split like never before and thus the sum as whole can never be used quite so effectively.

Politically, one has to be realistic and accept that a ban on betting on dog racing is unlikely, at least in my lifetime. While a necessary element in fully protecting greyhounds the arguments for, are complex and can in theory (though never in practice) be countered, and should it encompass horse racing? If not, why not? On the other hand there is a wealth of irrefutable evidence, even without publication of industry data, to support new statutory measures that outlaw dog racing on anything other than a straight course. It could be argued, with DEFRA balancing welfare and cost in the recent track legislation, this too has little chance of becoming law but dogs getting smashed up in the name of entertainment has no place in 21st century Britain. The subject must be tackled head on and it should be (for the antis) a priority in developing a political strategy, as is recognised by AFG. It would be nice - it is arguably a necessity - to have the backing of welfarists but the need to make our tracks safe is at least enjoying the support of one political party, albeit the Greens. Time now to convince the other parties.

We should further be calling for better enforcement of current legislation (to the shame not least of the RSPCA and LAs) but I also believe there is an interesting test case to be had on welfare law. When it can be expected that at any one race meeting two greyhounds will be injured, perhaps seriously, how does that fit with the requirement under Section 9 of the Animal Welfare Act 2006 that animals are "protected from pain, suffering [and] injury."[15-16] The above figure is the average given by the industry and thus what might it be for some tracks? In the survey I conducted on stewards' race comments 296 runners were recorded broke-down/lame over a 12-month period at Sittingbourne alone, to include 12 in a single meeting (see p. 44). In response DEFRA have said:

> We do not believe that the Animal Welfare Act effectively bans greyhound racing. The Act makes clear that Section 9 requires that those responsible for animals have to take such steps as are reasonable in all the circumstances to meet their welfare needs to the extent required by good practice. These circumstances are defined […] as including any lawful purpose for which an animal is kept. This section of the Act was drafted this way so as to avoid placing courts in a position where they may be asked to ban an activity by the back door. It provides a direction to the court that if an activity is lawful, the fact of its lawfulness should be taken into account.[15-17]

I agree it doesn't ban greyhound racing but that was never my thinking. Isn't there a case to be made against a trainer (the person responsible for the welfare of the animal) for entering a greyhound into a race when the risk of injury is substantial and the dog is seriously injured? Many a time, trainers have complained about a track for being unsafe but dogs are not withdrawn for fear of disciplinary action from racings' governing body. Can the legislation 'immunity clause' circumvent prosecution when any numbers of greyhounds are being injured on the track? I suspect the official answer to that is 'no'. I suspect in reality the answer is 'yes' and what we have is legalised animal abuse. The law should be amended and the 'immunity clause' removed, and as things stand it should be tested.

The rescues also have a part to play. Countless greyhounds are taken in every year bearing signs of neglect (if not cruelty) and yet it is my understanding very few trainers are ever reported to the RSPCA. Some might argue the RSPCA wouldn't take action anyway and I wouldn't disagree but every case, whatever the severity, should be brought to their attention. It should be on record and it may just influence RSPCA policy in favour of the greyhounds. Rescues should go further and publish all cases and what action the RSPCA have taken - if no action was taken, publish the fact. To say nothing is protecting those who ill-treat animals and serves only to perpetuate the suffering. Why for that matter are the stud books not reporting potential violations in breeding legislation to the relevant authorities? The above does raise interesting questions about the independence of groups, priorities and allegiances.

Solutions are neither quick nor easy. Raising awareness - the antis default position - is a vital component and yet reaching the public is a challenge in itself, and this is a movement taking on an industry that in a single marketing drive posted over one million pieces of promotional literature to addresses falling within the catchment area of tracks. The industry is today stemming the flow of blood and contrary to wishful thinking on the part of many antis is not on the brink of collapse, not that is the regulated sector. Most if not all flapping tracks are running at a loss and thus have a precarious future.

Ellesmere Port opened once again for business in March 2013 and is trying to defy the odds while the new track planned for Towcester Racecourse has yet to be constructed. Likely the next to fall by the wayside is Westhoughton in Lancashire. Landowner Sparkle Developments is looking to use the site for residential development and in May 2013 was (rather surprisingly) to contact antis for advice and support in closing down the stadium (previously met with local opposition). Councillors in late 2013 unanimously approved an application for 38 new homes. It is though the uncertain future of Wimbledon - the last of 33 tracks in London and home of the Derby - that is grabbing the headlines. Talk is of the historic ground being redeveloped for housing and a new football stadium, whereas would-be developer Paschal Taggart has plans to transform the site into the "Royal Ascot of dog racing." Interestingly he was reported saying: "I'm not going to make any money from this. I will end up with a bill for the greyhound track but my objective is to maintain racing."[15-18] The capital without greyhound racing would be a massive blow for the industry.

It is worthy also of note that the number of greyhounds *registered* annually for racing is now very similar to the mid-eighties (7,883 in 1985). The big difference today is the dogs are competing on fewer tracks and under fewer trainers. That has been the trend and in the not-too-distant future it will perhaps be just those tracks with a BAGS contract that survive, with any others having had the foresight to invest heavily in new facilities. Further, despite the best efforts of industry officials and the perplexing endorsement of welfarists, a black cloud now hangs over greyhound racing. In the decades ahead the biggest threat may simply come from a changing society; a society that is increasingly uncomfortable about animals being exploited in the name of entertainment. It is all well and good when runners are pets and competing on a straight course but not where runners are units, risking life and limb.

I have little doubt that eventually commercial operations will cease. It is just a question of when. Perhaps the last race will be nearer 2126 than 2026 but that is down not least to the antis and whether they can get their act together and be taken seriously. I would like to think the politicians will hasten its demise but how many have the courage to put welfare above economic considerations is questionable. What, however, the public can do is nothing - that is to say *never watch or bet on greyhound racing* - and in making that choice the misery endured by countless greyhounds will very quickly be confined to the history books. As someone who recognises greyhounds not as machines but as sentient beings that feel pain, and sense fear and crave affection, just as we do, that day cannot come soon enough.

References and notes

1-1   My concern was for a greyhound called Junior John running at Belle Vue and I was given to believe the dog had an eye problem. After making the enquiry Andrews' partner called back on three occasions, becoming increasing agitated and ultimately threatening. The fate of the dog isn't known.

2-1   Baker, N., "Going to the dogs - hostility to greyhound racing in Britain: puritanism, socialism and pragmatism," <u>Journal of Sport History</u>, Summer 1996, pp. 100-101

2-2   Newhouse, A., "How the NGRC has evolved," <u>The National Greyhound Racing Club 1928-2008</u>, (c. Dec.) 2008, p. 23

After serving 10 years with the Greyhound Express and 20 years as greyhound editor with The Sporting Life, Newhouse was appointed NGRC Chief Executive.

2-3   How independent is 'independent'? Assistant to the Chairman was Patrick Nixon, Secretary to the Bookmakers' Committee at the Horserace Betting Levy Board. Two of the three Assessors were Jim Cremin, greyhound editor with the Racing Post (following a career in greyhound racecourse management), and Jim Donnelley, Director of Racing and Sports Betting for PA Sport. Donoughue himself was hardly impartial when, in the preface, he declares "greyhound racing is a wonderful sport."

There was in the view of the RSPCA a "lack of real commitment in the Donoughue report to transparency and accountability."

Royal Society for the Prevention of Cruelty to Animals, <u>The Welfare of Racing Greyhounds - RSPCA Response to the APGAW and Donoughue Reports</u>, (c. 2008), p. 13

2-4   Data compiled using greyhound-data.com. The record on greyhound-data.com for races held in more recent years across British regulated tracks is *largely* complete and correct. I have though found much information on this site that is either misleading or inaccurate. Errors include wrong DOB, race comments mixed up and races in Ireland listed twice. Dogs with a change of name are also, on occasion, listed twice (a real problem in specific areas of research). It is also worth noting that the number of puppies recorded for any particular litter does not necessarily constitute the whole litter and not all litters (in part or whole) are recorded. That said it is still a very useful resource for information, perhaps the only resource for certain information.

3-1   Amphlett, F., "Greyhound racing - the real story," <u>Our Dogs</u>, 15 Aug. 2008, p. 22

3-2   Amphlett, F., "They walked away," <u>Greyhound Star</u>, Dec. 2011, p. 20

3-3   Newell. R., forum posting under "Greyhound homing scandal," #22, 11 Nov. 2007, Greyhoundscene, 13 Feb. 2012 <http://greyhoundscene.proboards.com/index.cgi?board=general&action=display&thread=6139&page=2>

The initial posting "Greyhound homing scandal" highlighted the practice of off-loading greyhounds onto literally anyone, and was subsequently censored by the site moderator. It generated 69 replies and 13 by breeder, trainer and owner Newell. As a long-standing member of the racing fraternity, initially in Britain and now Ireland, Newell's candid remarks carry much weight and included:

"I think you all live in cloud cuckoo land if you think there aren't hundreds of greys put to sleep before they even reach the track in the UK. Hundreds of pups are too slow to grade, some don't chase, others fight, injuries as pups etc. […]. I'd love to take out an anti down to the forest I go to every day with my pups in the hope my pups catch sight of something and chase it down and kill it. Sorry if that offends you but my pups are being bred to chase and hunt and eventually show enough courage on a track to go through the rigours of racing."

#19, 11 Nov. 2007

"I breed my pups. If they don't or can't race then they have to go. Hard but true and not easy for me to take that trip to the vets but alas it has to be done […]. There are still a great number of people, certainly in Ireland, that see their greys as livestock and no more than that. A few have them re-homed but the majority are put down after their use is over. Again, hard true fact."

#22, 11 Nov. 2007

3-4   Donoughue, B., <u>Independent Review of the Greyhound Industry in Great Britain</u>, Nov. 2007, p.12

3-5   In compiling information more recently on Peterson I had reason to question whether two of the trainer's dogs had, as stated on greyhound-data.com, been adopted through G4U. Debbie Buxcey (G4U founder) replied: "The dogs in question were on the G4U homing list as requested by their trainer. They subsequently disappeared from the trainer's kennels. I strongly recommend you speak to him about what happened to these dogs. We no longer home for this trainer as he did not fit into the G4U ethos; dogs disappearing being one point we disagreed on vehemently. The 'homed' button on Data was pressed instead of the 'delete' button - purely an administrative error."

E-mail, 28 Feb. 2012

3-6   At the time of writing 68 British based rescues alone list retired racers on greyhound-data.com as either available for adoption or adopted. A further section covers dogs homed directly/kept by their trainer/owner.

3-7   Telephone conversation, 7 Oct. 2009.

Argo Grace had a mouth full of rotten teeth and was reported to the RSPCA but by a member of the public and not Hebborn. It is understood no action was taken against Peterson. Hebborn further added: "They're meant to have had a vet's inspection but there's so many vets that don't even bother to go and have a look… The stipendiary steward is Colin Betteridge… I was only told the other day that he is useless. In all honesty he doesn't know anything, he wouldn't even know how to look at a dog."

3-8   "Disciplinary Committee Inquiries," 17 May 2012, Greyhound Board of

Great Britain, 5 Sep. 2013 <http://www.gbgb.org.uk/files/DC%20Findings _170512.pdf>

4-1 Telephone conversation, 17 Jan. 2011

Though Dawson was seemingly in violation of licence conditions, his establishment - Target Kennels - was a welcome sponsor for a new competition: British Bred Top Greyhound 2011.

4-2 Telephone conversation, 17 Jan. 2011

4-3 Clarification on the time frame - thought a maximum of 12 months - was sought from DEFRA but not provided. I got the impression the Department had no greater understanding of the legislation than local authorities.

4-4 Telephone conversation, 17 Jan. 2011

4-5 British Greyhound Racing Board, Regulations Pertaining to Greyhound Racing Under the Animal Welfare Act, (c. 2008), p. 2

5-1 Telephone conversation, 11 July 2007

The race track environment is a wholly unnatural environment for the greyhounds - a million miles from the open field of hare coursing. Many greyhounds are spooked and sometimes inured in non-racing related injuries. During a meeting at Owlerton (Sheffield) greyhounds ran onto the infield before Nervous Carla jumped the outer rail and took off at speed up steps and along the far side of the stadium. This ultimately led the greyhound onto an embankment and the roof of a dilapidated caravan where Carla, just 22 months young, plunged to the ground smashing both forelegs. The meeting carried on as normal.

5-2 "Frequently asked questions," Greyhound Board of Great Britain, 3 Apr. 2012 <http://www.gbgb.org.uk/FAQs.aspx>

5-3 "Adjournment (Summer)," Hansard, HC 17 July 2003, vol. 409 c. 513, 3 Apr. 2012 <http://hansard.millbanksystems.com/commons/2003/jul/17/ adjournment-summer#column_512>

5-4 AI (artificial insemination) is not recorded in the stud book for this mating and so *perhaps* it was not orchestrated (you would hope not). Looking through Volume 126, however, we have another litter recorded under Pickering where, if the information given is correct, the sire of the dam and litter is the same dog, and this litter is by way of AI (Larkhill Jo/Firehouse Jo, May 2005). One puppy from a total of three is recorded racing.

5-5 Telephone conversation, 7 Apr. 2009

5-6 This percentage would likely not be of surprise to certain industry officials but until publication by myself it was generally understood and accepted by all relevant groups, be they anti, 'pro' or sitting on the fence, that all non-graders were killed. I heard the Dogs Trust sought to verify it with the RGT and were given a revised figure of 20 percent. If true, the difference in what a high profile group and a member of public, off record so to speak, is being told is worthy of note. I will stick with 30 percent. Further, and while not in anyway scientific but interesting nevertheless, non-graders must account for at *least* 30 percent of the greyhounds I bump into when out walking (I always ask the owners about the history of their dogs).

6-1   Telephone conversation, 14 Jan. 2010

6-2   Kohnke, J., "Hock injuries," Greyhound Star, Nov. 2011, p. 9

6-3   Amphlett, F., "Alessandro Piras: vet on a mission," Greyhound Weekly, (c. Jan.) 2005

6-4   Atkinson, J., "Racing injuries," 12 June 2011, Easington Greyhounds, 17 May 2012 <http://www.easingtondogs.co.uk/racinginjuries.htm>

6-5   Telephone conversation, 12 Jan. 2010

6-6   Telephone conversation, 24 Jan. 2010

6-7   Though Emerson Brock was recorded broke-down and DNF he was said to be "absolutely fine." Brock, however, did not trial very well and a subsequent examination identified a torn muscle in the shoulder. Nothing too serious but the black male was later viciously attacked by another greyhound at trainer Jill Llewellin's kennels. It was an incident described by the trainer as a "challenge between the two as if to [see] who was going to be top dog." The other dog - also male and new to the kennels - targeted Brock's throat, explained Llewellin, who further added: "Being a nurse I thought I could treat him myself… but he sort of went downhill overnight and gradually lost consciousness. In the morning I took him to the vets and we said the best thing was to have him put down which was sad."

        Telephone conversation, 27 Apr. 2010

6-8   Telephone conversation, 5 Jan. 2010

6-9   Online news posting, 24 Sep. 2010, Greyhound Owners, Breeders and Trainers Association. URL not available

6-10   Swindon: Rackethall Kenny (7 July, 19.52, A3), Swift Abel (9 July, 18.11, A3), Wots Er Name (30 July, 22.15, A3) and Daytwo (31 July, 19.41, A8).

        Belle Vue: Clubbing Night (20 Aug., 21.25, A3), Sliding Bog (21 Aug., 20.20, A5) and Ballyverry Rock (28 Aug., 20.35, A1).

6-11   Benny, forum posting under "Injuries at Belle Vue," #2, 9 Oct. 2008, Belle Vue Owners Forum, URL not available (posting believed deleted)

6-12   Princess Rocket (16 May, 19.20, A9), Happy Hawk (29 May, 20.25, A3), Blue Fern (30 May, 21.35, A3), Liam Maldini (30 May, 22.35, A1), Dawn Sunset (1 June, trial) and Balreask Touch (11 June, 21.37, A2).

6-13   Agnew, B. P., "The nature and incidence of greyhound racing injuries," Fellowship thesis, Royal College of Veterinary Surgeons, Feb. 1992, p. 5

6-14   At the time of writing 68 British based rescues alone list retired racers on greyhound-data.com as either available for adoption or adopted. A further section covers dogs directly homed/kept by their trainer/owner.

6-15   The case of Our Vieri stands out in particular. Vieri crossed the line in second place with a respectable time of 26.56 for the standard distance at Harlow. The beautiful blue male was recorded "Blk1, Crd3, RnOn" (baulked turn 1, crowded turn 3 and ran on); nothing to give reason for concern but Vieri had fractured a hock. He was strapped up and carried to a waiting vehicle to be taken home but the owner then gave instruction for the animal to be destroyed.

6-16   Singleton, K., forum posting under "Track condition," #29, 4 Mar. 2010, Belle Vue Owners Forum, 29 May 2012 <http://bellevueowners.proboards. com/index.cgi?board=general&action=display&thread=16056>

6-17   Amphlett, F., "From the editors chair," <u>Greyhound Star</u>, Oct. 2011, p. 17

7-1   Smith, D., forum posting under "New track for Sheffield," 29 May 2008, Greyhoundscene, URL not available (posting believed deleted)

7-2   "Owlerton track is 'dangerous' for dogs - claim," <u>The Star</u>, 8 Aug. 2008, 14 June 2012 <http://www.thestar.co.uk/news/owlerton-track-is-dangerous-for-dogs-claim-1-251271>

7-3   Widerunner, forum posting under "Injuries at Sheffield," 10 July 2008, Greyhoundscene, 14 June 2012 <http://greyhoundscene.proboards.com/index.cgi?board=general&action=display&thread=18009>

7-4   Shoe, S., forum posting under "New track," #1, 26 May 2008, Greyhoundscene, 14 June 2012 <http://greyhoundscene.proboards.com/index.cgi?board=sheffield&action=display&thread=17182>

7-5   Maureenday, forum posting under "Was this a waste of £191,000?," #14, 12 Nov. 2010, Greyhoundscene, 14 June 2012 <http://greyhoundscene. proboards.com/index.cgi?board=general&action=display&thread=34855>

7-6   Craddock, J., "Ruined six meetings become unqualified Oxford nuisance," <u>Greyhound Star</u>, Mar. 2012, p. 31

7-7   Forbes, J., "New Newcastle racing surface," <u>Greyhound Star</u>, Mar. 2012, p. 33

7-8   Usherwood, J. R. and Wilson, A. M., "No force limit on greyhound sprint speed," <u>Nature</u>, 8 Dec. 2005, p. 753

7-9   Hercock, C. A., "Specialisation for fast locomotion: performance, cost and risk," PhD thesis, University of Liverpool, Sep. 2010, p. 206

7-10   Berg, M. S., "Radiographic, computed tomographic and histologic study of central tarsal bone fractures in racing greyhounds," MSc thesis, Ohio State University, 2008, p. 13

7-11   Dee, J. F. and Dee, L. G., "Fractures and dislocations associated with the racing greyhound," <u>Textbook of Small Animal Orthopaedics</u>, Ed. Newton, C. D. and Nunamaker, D. M., 1985, 26 June 2012 <http://cal.vet.upenn.edu/projects/saortho/chapter_35/35mast.htm>

7-12   Sweeney, P., "The increasing injury rate," <u>Greyhound Monthly</u>, June 2002, Greyhound Action, 26 June 2012 <http://www.greyhoundaction.org.uk/tracksoftears.html>

7-13   "Denis Beary on new Limerick's layout," 27 June 2010, Greyhound Owners, Breeders and Trainers Association, 26 June 2012 <http://www.gobata.co.uk/1/post/2010/06/denis-beary-on-new-limericks-layout.html>

7-14   Sweeney, P., "Greyhounds must have safer tracks," Sporting Press, 6 June 2002, 26 June 2012 <http://bgrd.co.uk/ugo/Safer%20Tracks.htm>

7-15   Gaisford, J., "Baiden is going round the bend," Oxford Mail, 24 July 2009, 4 July 2012 <http://www.oxfordmail.co.uk/sport/4511504.GREYHOUNDS__Baiden_is_going_round_the_bend/>

7-16   Kohnke, J., "Muscle injuries," Greyhound Star, Feb. 2012, p. 9

7-17   Johnston, A., forum posting under "Misuse of pups," 30 Nov. 2008, Greyhound Knowledge Forum, 4 July 2012 <http://greyhound-data.com/knowledge.php?b=4&note=420008>

7-18   Leeturnbull, forum posting under "Tonight," #5, 13 Aug. 2011, Belle Vue Owners Forum, 5 July 2012 <http://bellevueowners.proboards.com/index.cgi?board=general&action=display&thread=19238>

7-19   Watts, M., "Under the radar," Greyhound Star, Mar. 2012, p. 18

The above vet is one of four who attend on a professional basis Drumbo Park Greyhound Stadium in Northern Ireland where, at just *one race meeting* in July 2012, four greyhounds sustained hock fractures and were put to sleep.

7-20   Djdjdj, forum posting under "Injuries at Belle Vue," #14, 10 Oct. 2008, Belle Vue Owners Forum, URL not available (posting believed deleted)

7-21   Telephone conversation, 30 Oct. 2008

7-22   Hercock, C. A., "Specialisation for fast locomotion: performance, cost and risk," PhD thesis, University of Liverpool, Sep. 2010, p. 15

7-23   Amphlett, F., "From the editors chair," Greyhound Star, July 2012, p. 35

8-1   Amphlett, F., "Showme Thebunny at Sheffield for BBC Radio 5 Live," Greyhound Star, Sep. 2011, p. 15

8-2   An embarrassing exercise given a positive spin in the GBGB Annual Report 2011: "Further national exposure for the sport was welcomed in the form of Showme Thebunny […]. Linked to the SIS betting shop commentary, Colin Murray and regular guests Pat Nevin and Perry Groves cheered on the Norman Melbourne trained daughter of Westmead Hawk as she contested her races at Owlerton. Now happily retired, she was a great servant to the sport and helped to significantly raise its profile." You have to smile.

8-3   Baker, T., "The secret slaves of the dog racing industry," 2 Feb. 2012, Greyt Exploitations, 9 Aug. 2012 <http://www.greytexploitations.com/resources-and-reports/the-secret-slaves-of-the-dog-racing-industry>

8-4   Jeory, T., "Dog kennels branded 'disgusting'," Express.co.uk, 22 Jan. 2012, 9 Aug. 2012 <http://www.express.co.uk/posts/view/297147/Dog-kennels-branded-disgusting->

If Heaton's kennels are indeed inspected once a fortnight the trainer is being singled out for special treatment. Inspection by the area steward once or twice annually is nearer the mark.

8-5   Amphlett, F., "Board progress on £200,000 kennel improvement project," Greyhound Star, July 2012, p. 1

Believe industry spin and you might question the need for such a project: "Through administration of the well publicised Trainers Assistance Fund, the BGRB helps to ensure that all trainers are able to provide and maintain facilities that meet NGRC requirements, resulting in a high standard of welfare for greyhounds in their care."

British Greyhound Racing Board, Evidence for the Associate Parliamentary Group for Animal Welfare Enquiry into the Welfare of Racing Greyhounds in England, (c. 2006), p. 25

8-6   Royal Society for the Prevention of Cruelty to Animals, The Welfare of Racing Greyhounds - RSPCA Response to the APGAW and Donoughue Reports, (c. 2008), p. 11

8-7   Royal Society for the Prevention of Cruelty to Animals, The Welfare of Racing Greyhounds - RSPCA Response to the APGAW and Donoughue Reports, (c. 2008), p. 9

The section of the Act referenced covers England and Wales. Similar legislation exists in Scotland under the Animal Health and Welfare (Scotland) Act 2006, Section 24, and for Northern Ireland under the Welfare of Animals Act (Northern Ireland) 2011, Section 9.

8-8   "Kennel hand breaks silence on what's happening to dogs," mydogmagazine.com, (c. June 2009), 13 Aug. 2012 <http://mydogmagazine. com/dog-news/kennel-hand-breaks-silence-on-whats-happening-to-dogs/>

8-9   Telephone conversation, 19 Dec. 2008

8-10   Telephone conversation, 19 Dec. 2008

8-11   Amphlett, F., "They walked away," Greyhound Star, Dec. 2011, p. 21

8-12   Faughey, K., "Teesside greyhound trainer refutes neglect claims," gazettelive.co.uk, 5 Mar. 2010, 17 Aug. 2012 <http://www.gazettelive.co.uk/ news/teesside-news/2010/03/05/teesside-greyhound-trainer-refutes-neglect-claims-84229-25964728/>

8-13   "Aislaby greyhound kennels," e-mail to Declan Donnelly (Director of Regulation), cc. Clive Carr (Investigating Officer), 1 Dec. 2011

8-14   "Fwd: Aislaby greyhound kennels," e-mail to Declan Donnelly (Director of Regulation), cc. Greyhound Action, 6 Dec. 2011

8-15   Kohnke, J., "Winter warming," Greyhound Star, Jan. 2012, p. 9

8-16   "Amanda's diary," Greyhound Star, June 2011, p. 16

8-17   "Amanda's diary," Greyhound Star, July 2012, p. 12

8-18   Davis, S. and K., "Cornflake," The Race for Life, Autumn 2011, p. 13

Desperately wanting to help this poor greyhound, Sandra and Keith Davis tried repeatedly to buy the dog and in December 2010 a sale was agreed. The couple worked tirelessly to build her up both physically and emotionally and I would like to say that is where the story ends but Davis, K., being trainer, put her back on the track. The dog's improved condition was reflected in her grades but racing of course is not without risk. Mercifully, in June 2011 Cornflake (as she was affectionately known) was permanently retired and none the worse for the experience and has since been adopted.

8-19   "Appeal board hearings," 30 June 2008, National Greyhound Racing Club, URL not available

8-20   Telephone conversation, 30 Sep. 2008

If there was ever a case for a greyhound to be removed from the kennel environment and given special attention this was it. Sadly Pearly Black lost her life because she was a racing dog and not deserving of that attention.

8-21   "The truth about greyhound racing," Greyhound Board of Great Britain, 30 Aug. 2012 <http://www.gbgb.org.uk/TheTruthAboutRacing.aspx>

8-22   Horner, S., forum posting under "BVRGT, the jibes continue," #56*, 24 Mar. 2011, Belle Vue Owners Forum

*After I had referenced some of Horner's comments her posting was removed, likely to save the industry further embarrassment. The thread remains and what originally was posting #57 (and the initial response to Horner's posting) became #56.

8-23   "Amanda's Diary," Greyhound Star, July 2011, p. 16

8-24   "Disciplinary committee inquiries," 17 May 2012, Greyhound Board of Great Britain, 3 Sep. 2012 <http://www.gbgb.org.uk/files/DC%20Findings_170512.pdf>

9-1   "Help for mistreated greyhounds," Sunderland Echo, 21 Apr. 2012, 21 Sep. 2012 <http://www.sunderlandecho.com/news/local/all-news/help-for-mistreated-greyhounds-1-4469709>

A concerned member of the public, on reading about the greyhounds' neglect, e-mailed Morgan to ask whether either case had been brought to the attention of the RSPCA. Morgan made no comment.

9-2   Telephone conversation, 16 Sep. 2007

9-3   Burgoyne Bunny was subsequently homed through Yarmouth Greyhound Homefinders, I hope responsibly.

9-4   Telephone conversation, 11 Sep. 2007

9-5   McLean, A., "Utterly committed," The National Greyhound Racing Club 1928-2008, (c. Dec.) 2008, p. 3

9-6   Telephone conversation, 12 May 2010

9-7   The RGT's association with the regulatory authority does, I believe, make this a viable proposal though in an ideal world I would sooner home checks were carried out by non-RGT greyhound-specific rescues. Opponents might argue it would increase the number of greyhounds euthanased; a possibility that says much about their owners. Of course if good provision cannot be made for the dogs, owners should not be involved in the 'sport' and it is for the regulatory body to safeguard their welfare. The proposal gains greater viability in the light of a recent study of performance data for racing bitches: "The detailed analysis produced compelling evidence that spaying has little or no loss in a bitch's performance and led to the WSC [GBGB Welfare Standing Committee] recommending spaying as a safe alternative to oestrus suppression or seasonal rest." This in turn it was recognised has the benefit of "speed and cost savings when it comes to homing the greyhound."

"Benefits of spaying a greyhound bitch," Greyhound Star, Nov. 2012, p. 15

10-1   "Remember when in: July," Greyhound Star, July 2012, pp. 10-11

10-2   Mehta, A., "Dogs left to suffer in squalid conditions," Peterborough Telegraph, 28 Apr. 2008, 29 Oct. 2012 <http://www.peterboroughtoday.co. uk/news/environment/dogs-left-to-suffer-in-squalid-conditions-1-98456>

10-3   "Greyhound track 'conditions poor'," BBC News, 29 Oct. 2009, 30 Oct. 2012 <http://news.bbc.co.uk/1/hi/wales/south_west/8332622.stm>

10-4   "Dog trainer sentenced for neglect," BBC News, 22 Feb. 2010, 31 Oct. 2012 <http://news.bbc.co.uk/1/hi/england/merseyside/8528041.stm>

10-5   Stewart, G., "Birkenhead greyhound trainer Ian Street admits animal cruelty charges," LiverpoolEcho.co.uk, 22 Jan. 2010, 31 Oct. 2012 <http://www. liverpoolecho.co.uk/liverpool-news/local-news/2010/01/22/birkenhead-greyhound-trainer-ian-street-admits-animal-cruelty-charges-100252-25657708/>

10-6   Hore, J., "Greyhound trainer locked up for cruelty," EDP 24, 20 Mar. 2009, 1 Nov. 2012 <http://www.edp24.co.uk/news/greyhound_trainer_locked_up_for _cruelty_1_170966>

10-7   "Dogs died in agony in Grantham house," GranthamJournal.co.uk, 30 Aug. 2011, 5 Nov. 2012 <http://www.granthamjournal.co.uk/news/local/dogs-died-in-agony-in-grantham-house-1-3010220>

10-8   "Man admits animal cruelty over greyhound deaths," BBC News Lincolnshire, 21 Sep. 2011, 5 Nov. 2012 <http://www.bbc.co.uk/news/uk-england-lincolnshire-15012902>

10-9   Carr, who operated under the name Osiris Greyhounds, is registered with the NCC as the breeder for a mating between Final Nijinsky/I Hope So (August 2009 (four dogs/two bitches)).

Carr and Campbell are registered with the NCC as breeders for a mating between 1) Fear Haribo/Glengar Tara (August 2009 (four dogs/two bitches)) and 2) Setemup Joe/Glengar Tara (December 2007 (one dog)).

Carr was registered with the NCC as the owner for Final Nijinsky and I Hope So.

Carr and Campbell were registered with the NCC as owners for Babyalahs Gold, Glengar Tara, Salems Hero and Babyalah.

Two videos (on YouTube) include a more recent mating and there are further greyhounds that I understand were registered with the ICC.

10-10   Foggo, D., "Pet home 'a conveyor belt of killing'," The Sunday Times, 17 Sep. 2006

10-11   Foggo, D., "Killing field of the dog racing industry," The Sunday Times, 16 July 2006

10-12   "Man fined over greyhound deaths," BBC News, 16 Mar. 2007, 14 Nov. 2012 <http://news.bbc.co.uk/1/hi/england/wear/6457185.stm>

Andre Menache - a veterinary surgeon with 30 years' experience - said of the use of bolt guns: "Occasionally an animal may regain consciousness after the initial concussion. This is especially likely if an animal moves its head at the instant the pistol is discharged. Worse still, the operator may inflict a serious wound without hitting the brain at all and be faced with a completely conscious animal in agony. In a successful stun, although brain matter may have been destroyed the brain stem is often left intact, which explains why the heart will continue to beat. Although this may be desirable in a slaughterhouse context, in the case of dogs it necessitates the need for a supplementary agent such as a lethal injection with barbiturates to ensure swift euthanasia."

Menache, A., "Captive bolt guns have no place in our 21st century society," 17 June 2009

The above leaves you wondering how many of those greyhounds taken to Smith were buried alive.

10-13   Foggo, D., "Knacker's yard disposes of unwanted greyhounds for £20," The Sunday Times, 2 Nov. 2008

10-14   Henley, J., "Going to the dogs," The Guardian, 9 Aug. 2008, 12 Nov. 2012 <http://www.guardian.co.uk/uk/2008/aug/09/london.greyhoundracing>

10-15   Jeory, T., "Agony of caged greyhounds," Express.co.uk, 30 May 2010, 7 Nov. 2012 <http://www.express.co.uk/posts/view/178015/Agony-of-caged-greyhounds>

10-16   Foggo, D., "Greyhound breeder offers slow dogs to be killed for research," The Sunday Times, 11 May 2008

In the survey I conducted on greyhound puppies unaccounted for only 45 percent of Pickering's dogs reached naming stage and a mere 23 percent were recorded racing.

10-17   Foggo, D., "Vets' secret trade in body parts," The Sunday Times, 2 Mar. 2008

10-18   "Greyhound found with ears cut off," BBC News, 24 Apr. 2009, 16 Nov. 2012 <http://news.bbc.co.uk/1/hi/england/tyne/8017738.stm>

10-19   "Appeal over stranded greyhound," Northumberland Gazette, 28 May 2009

10-20   "Greyhound just 'days from death'," BBC News, 8 July 2009, 19 Nov. 2012 <http://news.bbc.co.uk/1/hi/scotland/edinburgh_and_east/8140539.stm>

10-21   "Shock over injured dog," This is Grimsby, 20 June 2009, 19 Nov. 2012 <http://www.thisisgrimsby.co.uk/Shock-injured-dog/story-11537387-detail/story.html>

I took it upon myself to try and find out what I could about this greyhound. His racing name was Hampsey, he was born 6 April 2006 and the last *registered* owner was James McCorry from County Antrim. McCorry said the dog was sold for next to nothing to someone at his local track who in turn sold the dog within a matter of days through an auction at Armadale flapping track (West Lothian). The trail then goes cold. A person with a professional connection to the track made inquiries on my behalf but of course it's a world in which people protect each other or simply are too frightened to speak out.

10-22   Chapman, T., "Ex-racing greyhound found dumped," News Guardian, 2 Oct. 2012, 20 Nov. 2012 <http://www.newsguardian.co.uk/news/local/ex-racing-greyhound-found-dumped-video-1-4984321>

10-23   "Injured racing dog left to die," Wigantoday.net, 29 Mar. 2012, 20 Nov. 2012 <http://www.wigantoday.net/news/local-news/injured-racing-dog-left-to-die-1-4395715>

10-24   Watson, P., "Dead greyhound horror discovery," Hartlepool Mail, 16 Mar. 2009, 21 Nov. 2012 <http://www.hartlepoolmail.co.uk/news/local/dead-greyhound-horror-discovery-1-1036321>

10-25   "Greyhound dumped in Bristol 'with ears cut off'," This is Bristol, 11 Mar. 2009, 21 Nov. 2012 <http://www.thisisbristol.co.uk/Greyhound-dumped-Bristol-ears-cut/story-11295485-detail/story.html>

10-26   McLaughlin, D., "Czech group offers new lease of life for greyhounds destroyed in retirement," The Irish Times, 30 Mar. 2012, 23 Nov. 2012 <http://www.irishtimes.com/newspaper/ireland/2012/0330/1224314099855.html>

10-27   Swords, W., "Discarded dogs given just one hour to live in shelter," The Irish Mail on Sunday, 24 June 2012, p. 32

Table of pound figures: Animals Need a Voice in Legislation

10-28   "Greyhound is mutilated and left for dead," Banbridge Leader, 16 Dec. 2009, 27 Nov. 2012 <http://www.banbridgeleader.co.uk/news/local/greyhound-is-mutilated-and-left-for-dead-1-1634406>

10-29   Collins, D., "Greyhound abandoned with ears cut off," Irish Examiner, 14 Apr. 2006, Greyhound Action, 27 Nov. 2012 <http://www.greyhoundaction.org.uk/iirelandnewsnews.html#moreMutil>

10-30   Tighe, M., "Mutilated greyhound heralds tighter controls," Sunday Times (Ireland), 17 June 2007, Greyhound Action, 28 Nov. 2012 <http://www.greyhoundaction.org.uk/iirelandnewsnews.html#aoife>

10-31   Nolan, D., "Gardai baffled over 'sick' scene of animal cruelty," The

Kerryman, 21 Dec. 2006, Greyhound Action, 29 Nov. 2012 <http://www.greyhoundaction.org.uk/iirelandnewsnews.html>

10-32   "Dead dog dumping ground sparks probe," Irish Examiner, 19 Mar. 2008, Greyhound Action, 29 Nov. 2012 <http://www.greyhoundaction.org.uk/iirelandnewsnews.html>

10-33   Clancy, P., "Bodies of mutilated dogs found in river," The Irish Times, 1 Aug. 2008

10-34   "Dog's 'disgusting death the tip of the iceberg'," Derry Journal, 6 Mar. 2009, 5 Dec. 2012 <http://www.derryjournal.com/news/local/dog-s-disgusting-death-the-tip-of-the-iceberg-1-2135487>

10-35   McDonald, B., "Mutilated remains of greyhounds dumped at popular pier," Independent.ie, 3 June 2009, 5 Dec. 2012 <http://www.independent.ie/national-news/mutilated-remains-of-greyhounds-dumped-at-popular-pier-1759326.html>

10-36   Fleming, M., "Cruelty and neglect: the tragic fate of the dogs who race for their lives," Irish Daily Mail, 10 July 2010, p. 11

10-37   "Hounded," BBC Radio Ulster, 18 Mar. 2012, YouTube, 6 Dec. 2012 <http://www.youtube.com/watch?v=T7hiWRtWUb8>

10-38   Fitzgerald, A., "Owners of greyhounds slaughtered in Limerick are tracked," Limerick Leader, 13 Apr. 2012, 10 Dec. 2012 <http://www.limerickleader.ie/news/local/owners-of-greyhounds-slaughtered-in-limerick-are-tracked-1-3724169#>

10-39   Meneely, G., "Greyhound slaughter," Irish Sun, 21 May 2009, p. 11

10-40   Mooney, J., "Chinese set to take away Irish dogs," The Sunday Times, 27 Feb. 2011

10-41   Beazley, M., "Future of greyhounds in China," The Irish Times, 4 Mar. 2011

10-42   Carbery, G., "Assurances on export of greyhounds to China," The Irish Times, 3 May 2011

10-43   Carbery, G., "Greyhound export plan shelved," The Irish Times, 4 May 2011

Being looked at was the development of about five greyhound tracks in China, operated on 25-year contracts.

10-44   Parry, S., "The dogs who run for their lives," Irish Daily Mail, 7 May 2011

10-45   Deegan, G., "Animal welfare concerns stall greyhound board's China plan," Independent.ie, 30 Mar. 2012, 17 Dec. 2012 <http://www.independent.ie/national-news/animal-welfare-concerns-stall-greyhound-boards-china-plan-3066478.html>

11-1   "Perfect pets racing into their owners' affections," Independent.ie, 15 May 2012, 8 Jan. 2013 <http://www.independent.ie/lifestyle/perfect-pets-racing-into-their-owners-affections-3108924.html>

11-2   "Greyhound welfare at the heart of new initiatives," Joe.ie, 1 Dec. 2011, 8

Jan. 2013 <http://www.joe.ie/sports/greyhounds/greyhound-welfare-at-the-heart-of-new-initiatives-0018191-1>

11-3   An indication on the proportion of litters bred in relation to hare coursing was sought from the ICC who said: "We do not differentiate between coursing and track litters and could not hazard a guess as to the percentage."

E-mail, 17 Jan. 2013

11-4   "Amanda's diary," <u>Greyhound Star</u>, Mar. 2012, p. 12

11-5   Kohnke, J., "The vet's clinic," <u>Greyhound Star</u>, Mar. 2012, p. 9

The use of either a strap muzzle or electric collar is of course deplorable. On the former veterinarian and Greyhound Star columnist Michael Watts said the following: "One trainer of my acquaintance used to put strap muzzles on all the noisy inmates of his kennels. Tying a dog's mouth shut will surely stop him barking but it also stops him from drinking when he feels thirsty and from panting on hot days and so can contribute to physical ill health as well as the incalculable ill-effects it doubtless has on his mental well-being. One look [at] the frightened eyes of those poor mute dogs was enough for me and I swore never to set foot in the man's yard again."

"Under the radar," <u>Greyhound Star</u>, Apr. 2012, p.14

11-6   Due to the training and treatment of racing dogs, and the rigours of competing on the track, a retired greyhound *may* require more time, patience and understanding than other breeds. You would, however, be forgiven for thinking otherwise. Further, wire fencing, ruts and pots holes are just a few of many hazards that are potentially lethal to greyhounds because of their speed. Again, you would be forgiven for thinking otherwise. The dogs are 'sold' as '40 mph couch potatoes' that require just two 20 minute walks a day. Indeed I have even seen it said that just one 20 minute walk per day or two 15 minutes walks is fine. The IGB's Welfare Manager, Barry Coleman, is on record saying: "Once they retire, they would prefer a sofa than going out for a run, so they actually don't need much exercise. That makes them great for people who work, as greyhounds are happy to sleep for much of the day."[11-1] As someone who has adopted greyhounds for a mere 25 years I can tell you that greyhounds do not like to be left alone for long periods of time and, where health and/or age does not dictate otherwise, enjoy walks longer than 20 minutes. The key point is greyhounds end up in homes not suitable and perhaps with caring owners but who are unable to cope, and due to ignorance about the breed pet greyhounds incur serious injuries - sometimes fatal - in avoidable 'accidents'. The homing of greyhounds independently has been covered but what of the rescues? Some are very responsible but is it a numbers' game with others? It is important for both the owners and dogs that people looking to adopt are given all relevant information though I must further add greyhounds can and *do make wonderful pets*.

12-1   "Amanda's Diary," <u>Greyhound Star</u>, Mar. 2012, p.12

12-2   "Memorandum submitted by Lord Lipsey, Chairman, British Greyhound Racing Board," 25 Aug. 2004, Select Committee on Environment, Food and Rural Affairs, 4 Feb. 2013 <http://www.publications.parliament.uk/pa/

cm200405/cmselect/cmenvfru/52/4091608.htm>

12-3   Craddock, J., "Big dogging event attracts plenty of Monmore interest," Greyhound Star, Nov. 2011, p. 39

12-4   Amphlett, F., "Industry needs to learn from Hearn," Greyhound Star, Dec. 2012, p. 38

12-5   Amphlett, F., "From the editors chair," Greyhound Star, Sep. 2011, p. 17

12-6   It was interesting to read that the "National Association of Dog Wardens were given the 'Data Protection runaround' by the BGRB when they were trying to trace the owners of abandoned greyhounds."[12-5] While names of owners would be covered by the Act, to not assist wardens on such matters beggars belief.

12-7   Telephone conversation, (c. Feb.) 2007

12-8   Associate Parliamentary Group for Animal Welfare, The Welfare of Greyhounds, May 2007, p. 32

12-9   Department for Environment, Food and Rural Affairs, Summary of Responses to the Consultation on the Welfare of Racing Greyhounds Regulations 2010 from 30 April 2009 to 22 July 2009, Oct. 2009, pp. 38-39

12-10   Department for Environment, Food and Rural Affairs, Summary of Responses to the Consultation on the Welfare of Racing Greyhounds Regulations 2010 from 30 April 2009 to 22 July 2009, Oct. 2009, p. 37

12-11   GREY2K USA, "Greyhounds suffer serious injuries," Greyhound Racing in Arizona, Feb. 2011, p. 7

12-12   Department for Environment, Food and Rural Affairs, "Impact assessment of regulations to promote the welfare of racing greyhounds," Consultation on the Welfare of Racing Greyhounds Regulations 2010, Apr. 2009, pp. 12-13

12-13   Greyhound Board of Great Britain, Annual Report 2009, p. 12

12-14   Hookham, M., "Why Annette has grave doubts about greyhound track," Liverpool Daily Post, 13 May 2003, 14 Feb. 2013 <http://www. liverpooldailypost.co.uk/liverpool-news/regional-news/2003/05/13/why-annette-has-grave-doubts-about-greyhound-track-99623-12952442/>

        Perhaps the GRA 'expert' was not aware racing dogs are reaching their maximum speed within about 20 metres of jumping the traps, or could it be the drivel was fuelled by commercial considerations?

12-15   "Greyhound welfare campaigners promise ongoing campaign at Towcester Racecourse," Advertiser and Review (Bicester), 1 May 2012, 14 Feb. 2013 <http://www.buckinghamtoday.co.uk/news/local/greyhound-welfare-campaigners-promise-ongoing-campaign-at-towcester-racecourse-1-3793956>

12-16   Scase, D., forum posting under "Beware of 'odd' phone call," #6, 21 Oct. 2008, Greyhoundscene, URL not available (posting believed deleted)

12-17   Online news postings, 28 Sep. 2010, Greyhound Owners, Breeders and

Trainers Association. URL not available

12-18   Online news postings, 24 Sep. 2010, Greyhound Owners, Breeders and
         Trainers Association. URL not available

12-19   Greyhound Board of Great Britain, Annual Report 2009, p. 1

12-20   Trew, J., "Re: Request for information about greyhounds for my GCSE
         studies," e-mail to Beth Fowler, 17 Jan. 2013

12-21   Smith, D., forum posting under "Eve Blanchard kennels," #186 (originally
         #188), 24 Jan. 2009, Greyhoundscene, 26 Feb. 2013 <http://greyhoundscene.
         Proboards.com/index.cgi?board=general&action=display&thread=21086&
         page=13>

12-22   Smith, D., forum posting under "Eve Blanchard kennels," #189 (originally
         #191), 24 Jan. 2009, Greyhoundscene, 26 Feb. 2013 <http://greyhoundscene.
         Proboards.com/index.cgi?board=general&action=display&thread=21086&
         page=13>

12-23   "Out of the race," The Telegraph, 22 Jan. 2000, 27 Feb. 2013 <http://www.
         therockfollies.co.uk/Out%20of%20the%20race.htm>

12-24   British Greyhound Racing Board, Greyhound Welfare: A Briefing for
         Members of the All Party Parliamentary Greyhound Group, Oct. 2008, p. 4

         Purpose of the APPGG: "To raise parliamentary awareness of issues relating
         to the greyhound industry and to promote the sport."

         Benefits the APPGG receive from outside parliament: The "Greyhound
         Board of Great Britain provides administrative support to the group and also
         funds travel to, and dinner and racing at, occasional race events."

         "Register of All-Party Groups: Greyhound," 19 Mar. 2013, 5 Apr. 2013
         <http://www.publications.parliament.uk/pa/cm/cmallparty/register/
         greyhound.htm>

12-25   Almroth-Wright, I., "Is the end nigh for dog racing?", BBC News, 12 Jan.
         2013, 28 Feb. 2013 <http://www.bbc.co.uk/news/uk-england-20968535>

12-26   Whittaker, F., "Fear for greyhounds if stadium is closed," Oxford Mail, 14
         Aug. 2012, 28 Feb. 2013 <http://www.oxfordmail.co.uk/news/9871318.
         Fear_for_greyhounds_if_stadium_is_closed/?action=success>

12-27   Amphlett, F., "An inside glimpse of the Greyhound Forum," Greyhound Star,
         Jan. 2013, p. 21

12-28   Baker, D. (Chief Executive, Wood Green), letter to Action for Greyhounds,
         13 Sep. 2002

12-29   "Greyhound Welfare Working Group," minutes, 25 Apr. 2006

12-30   Amphlett, F., "An inside glimpse of the Greyhound Forum," Greyhound Star,
         Jan. 2013, p. 20

12-31   "Supplementary memorandum submitted by the British Greyhound Racing
         Board," Oct. 2004, Select Committee on Environment, Food and Rural

Affairs, 12 Mar. 2013 <http://www.publications.parliament.uk/pa/cm200405/cmselect/cmenvfru/52/4091613.htm>

12-32   Binns, D., "'Back Stow housing plans' say animal rights campaigners," Guardian (Chingford), 1 Aug. 2011, 13 Mar. 2013 <http://www.guardian-series.co.uk/news/9171357.CHINGFORD___Back_Stow_housing_plans__say_animal_rights_campaigners/>

12-33   Bishop, L. B. (Mayoral Administrator, Wolverhampton City Council), "Christmas party at the dogs," e-mail to Plumridge and Green, 21 Sep. 2011

12-34   Baker, N., "Going to the dogs - hostility to greyhound racing in Britain: puritanism, socialism and pragmatism," Journal of Sport History, Summer 1996, p. 101

12-35   "Owlerton stadium raises money for local charity," Postcode Gazette, 4 Apr. 2012, 15 Mar. 2013 <http://postcodegazette.com/news/9001709752/owlerton-stadium-raises-money-for-local-charity-AT-sheffield-owlerton-greyhound-stadium-sheffield/>

12-36   "Cashing and dashing for kids at Shawfield," Greyhound Star, July 2012, p.33

12-37   Amphlett, F., "From the editors chair," Greyhound Star, Dec. 2012, p. 35

12-38   Amphlett, F., "From the editors chair," Greyhound Star, Sep. 2011, p. 17

12-39   The Alan Titchmarsh Show, ITV, 3 Oct. 2011, YouTube, 20 Mar. 2013 <https://www.youtube.com/watch?v=6sTuHYZE7R4>

12-40   Tampeters, forum posting under "Titchmarsh you winker," 3 Oct. 2011, Greyhoundscene, 20 Mar. 2013 <http://greyhoundscene.proboards.com/index.cgi?board=general&action=display&thread=41295>

12-41   Trap to line, forum posting under "Titchmarsh you winker," #20, 3 Oct. 2011, Greyhoundscene, 20 Mar. 2013 <http://greyhoundscene.proboards.com/index.cgi?board=general&action=display&thread=41295&page=2>

12-42   Action for Greyhounds, "Peaceful protestors shot at - Yarmouth greyhound racing stadium," press release, 19 Aug. 2003

12-43   Binns, D., "Man cautioned over councillor death threats," Guardian (Waltham Forest), 16 May 2012, 26 Mar. 2013 <http://www.guardian-series.co.uk/your_local_areas/9708450.WALTHAM_FOREST__Man_cautioned_over_councillor_death_threats/>

12-44   "Councillor Pye," 14 May 2012, Save Our Stow, 26 Mar. 2013 <http://saveourstow.wordpress.com/2012/05/14/councillor-pye/>

13-1   "Cruelty to greyhounds," Hansard, HC 7 Feb. 1994, vol. 237 c. 119, 11 Apr. 2013 <http://hansard.millbanksystems.com/commons/1994/feb/07/cruelty-to-greyhounds>

13-2   Brown, J., "A dog's life ain't what it used to be," The Independent, 17 Jan. 2005, 18 Apr. 2013 <http://www.independent.co.uk/news/uk/this-britain/a-dogs-life-aint-what-it-used-to-be-486989.html>

Rusty was found severely injured on a rubbish tip in South Wales. Following a toe injury that terminated the dog's career on the track, Andrew Gough (for the sum of £10) shot Rusty in the head with a bolt gun and cut his ears off to prevent identification from tattoo markings. Despite the appalling injuries, the black male was still alive and conscious when found but could not be saved. A vet humanely ended the animal's suffering.

13-3   "Greyhound Action on the up," Running For Their Lives, Mar. Apr. 2009, p. 1

13-4   At the time of writing more e-mails arrive on my desk concerning Trudy Baker:

"I think more people are realising what she is up to, trying to control everyone who gets involved with the campaign, then falling out with and slagging off anyone who doesn't agree with her or doesn't want to work with her."

"Re: CSSC civil servant and Baker," e-mail, 6 May 2013

"I'm afraid that despicable 'B' is just out of control and is in danger of doing more damage to the campaign than she already has - if that's possible - unless more people, who know the truth about her, will actually stand up and deal with the issue. […]. The level of her insults are also worthy of an ignorant foul-mouthed guttersnipe and do nothing to make the anti-racing campaign look either professional or intelligent."

"New messages" (Facebook), e-mail, 6 May 2013

13-5   Baker, T., "Re: Proposed welfare regulations - unenforceable and worthless," e-mail to Sighthound Mail, cc. Greyhound Action, South West Animal Protection, 9 Dec. 2009

13-6   "Welcome to Greyt Exploitations," Greyt Exploitations, 30 Apr. 2013 <http://www.greytexploitations.com/>

13-7   "A Question of Sport?," Greyt Exploitations, 1 May 2013 <http://www.greytexploitations.com/resources-and-reports/a-question-of-sport>

13-8   "Update," 26 Mar. 2010, Greyt Exploitations, 2 May 2013 <http://www.greytexploitations.com/resources-and-reports/did-the-bbc-callously-dismiss-the-deaths-of-two-greyhounds>

13-9   Hespe, C., e-mail to Greyhound Action, 20 Nov. 2010

13-10   "Goodbye from Greyhound Action: Operations ended as part of efficiency move," 27 May 2011, Greyhound Action, 14 May 2013 <http://greyhound-action.blogspot.co.uk/>

13-11   Hespe, C., e-mail to Greyhound Action, 17 Nov. 2010

13-12   Coates, J., "Ears ripped off and bothered: cruel fate of retired greyhounds," Express.co.uk, 20 May 2012, 16 May 2013 <http://www.express.co.uk/news/uk/321233/Ears-ripped-off-and-bothered-cruel-fate-of-retired-greyhounds>

13-13   "Thousands of racing greyhounds 'vanish' each year," BBC News Northern Ireland, 16 Mar. 2012, 17 May 2013 <http://www.bbc.co.uk/news/uk-

northern-ireland-17396205>

13-14   Smith, S., "Happy to see an end to cruel greyhound racing," Oxford Mail, 3 Jan. 2013, 20 May 2013 <http://www.oxfordmail.co.uk/yoursay/letters/ 10136791.Happy_to_see_an_end_to_cruel_greyhound_races/>

13-15   "A night at Belle Vue 'dog' track," photograph, 19 Apr. 2012, Facebook/Greyt Exploitations, 21 May 2013 <https://www.facebook.com/ greyt.exploitations>

13-16   "New survey brings into question the fate of thousands of greyhound pups: GA comment," (c. Apr.) 2009, Greyhound Action, 22 May 2013 <http:// www.greyhoundaction.org.uk/tracksoftears.html>

13-17   The industry has provided modest grants to a small number of independent rescues through the establishment of the Retired Greyhound Fund (20 grants totalling £26,000 in 2011 (towards capital projects)). Funding for the RGT, by way of the BGRF, was £1.4 million in 2012 (accounting for 39 percent of the charity's incoming resources).

13-18   The Racing Dog Protection Act 2009 was put together by new 'group' Society for the Prevention of Cruelty to Racing Animals. It was said: "An Act to make provision about racing with dogs; to prohibit the commercial element (betting on the outcome of the races)." Endorsements were received from a number of organisations to include the World Society for the Protection of Animals, People for the Ethical Treatment of Animals, and Animal Aid.

13-19   Green Party policy AR418: "The Green Party will end the exploitation of animals in horse racing, greyhound racing and all situations where animals are commercially raced. There would be an immediate ban on the use of the whip in horse racing and in jumps racing, *and on the use of a non-linear track in greyhound racing* [emphasis added]. A single regulatory authority would be put in place for each sport, tasked with establishing and enforcing strict welfare standards. There would be a requirement for full traceability of all animals involved in racing throughout their lives (using microchip technology where applicable) and full publication of injury and death statistics. These statistics would be used as evidence to close dangerous tracks and ban trainers with poor records. Breeding and import of animals for racing will be tightly regulated and monitored to improve welfare and prevent over-breeding. There would be regulation on the conditions and times of transportation of animals used in sport as well as the housing of all animals. A high level of compulsory levy would be imposed on all betting, to be used solely for welfare improvements."

"Animal rights: Policies," Green Party, 3 June 2013 <http://policy.greenparty .org.uk/ar>

The wording is not very clear but what is meant by "non-linear" is anything other than a straight course (verified by the Green Party).

13-20   Since the formation of GREY2K USA in 2001 the decline in American dog racing has been dramatic to say the least - 49 tracks in 15 states reduced to 22 tracks in seven states by 2013 - though it should be noted the circumstances in America are very different to that of Britain. Bizarrely GREY2K and track owners became allies in the need to decouple racing from more lucrative casino operations. Owners had secured licences to operate slot machines and poker tables on the condition a percentage of profits would subsidise the dogs. The indoor gaming side has since proved far more popular than dog racing and thus an ever-increasing number of owners are wanting either to reduce the scale of live racing or shut down tracks. The subject is covered well in an article in The New York Times: "Greyhound races face extinction at the hands of casinos they fostered," 8 Mar. 2012.

In October 2013, GREY2K USA was relaunched as GREY2K USA Worldwide, as part of new initiatives to combat greyhound abuse on a global scale.

14-1   Voluntary measures as laid down in the Charter for the Racing Greyhound:

●The registered owner and/or keeper of a greyhound should take full responsibility for the physical and mental well-being of the greyhound and should do so with full regard to the dog's future welfare.

●All greyhounds should be permanently identified and properly registered with relevant records kept by the owner and/or keeper.

●All greyhounds should be fully vaccinated by a veterinary surgeon and provided with a current Certificate of Vaccination.

●All greyhounds must be provided with suitable food and accommodation and have unrestricted access to clean fresh water.

●Adequate arrangements must be made to allow for exercise and socialisation.

●Breeding and rearing: over-production of greyhounds through indiscriminate breeding must be avoided. Where a racing greyhound is bred from, the long term welfare of the bitch and puppies must be paramount.

●Training must be conducted so as to safeguard the long term welfare of the dog.

●Where destruction is inevitable, greyhounds should be euthanased humanely by the intravenous injection of a suitable drug administered under the supervision of a veterinary surgeon.

●When transported all greyhounds should do so in safety and comfort.

●All tracks should appoint a member of staff responsible for animal welfare.

●A supervising veterinary surgeon must be present whenever greyhounds are raced at tracks.

●Tracks and kennels must be designed and maintained to ensure the highest welfare standards for the racing greyhound.

●Greyhounds must only race if passed fit by a veterinary surgeon immediately prior to racing.

●Greyhounds must be entitled to receive emergency veterinary care if injured.

●Drugs which may affect the performance of a greyhound when racing should not be permitted.

●The industry must endeavour to ensure that all racecourses have a properly funded home-finding scheme for retired greyhounds in operation. Such schemes should work closely with other welfare and charitable bodies seeking to find good homes for ex-racing greyhounds.

Covering absolute minimum standards one would expect for racing dogs the production of the Charter said much about their care… or should say, lack of it. Even today, there are measures laid down in the Charter that, universally, remain only an aspiration.

14-2   Dogs Trust, Greyhounds Questions – Responses, 2009, p. 1

14-3   Dogs Trust, Greyhounds Questions – Responses, 2009, p. 8

14-4   "UKAS committee update," Aug. 2010, 20 June 2013 <http://www.gbgb
        .org.uk/files/UKAS%20Committee%20web%20update%20August.pdf>

14-5   "From the editors chair," Greyhound Star, Oct. 2011, p. 17

14-6   Binns, D., "Welfare groups downplay Stow racing bid involvement,"
        Guardian (Chingford), 5 Aug. 2011, 21 June 2013 <http://www.guardian-
        series.co.uk/news/9180949.CHINGFORD__Animal_welfare_groups_
        downplay_involvement_with_Stow_racing_bid/>

14-7   Dixon. J. (Online Communication's Officer), "Re: Phone call," e-mail to
        Sighthound Mail, 2 Aug. 2011

14-8   Taylor, S. (Head of Campaigns and Communications), "Re: Greyhounds," e-
        mail to Sighthound Mail, 20 Oct. 2011

14-9   It is evident from reading further that 'UK' is reference to litters recorded
        with the Greyhound Stud Book. In vol. 131 (entries received June 2011-May
        2012), 312 litters are detailed, equating to 1,966 puppies, and about half that
        figure are likely to fail grading. We have to go back to the year 2003-4 for
        the puppies total to reach and exceed 5,000 (and thus arrive at a figure of
        2,500 for non-graders).

14-10   Westmore, L. (Campaign/PR Co-ordinator), letter to Action for Greyhounds,
        2 Sep. 2003

14-11   "Why greyhound cruelty is wrong" (a not very well-thought out title by the
        League for this page: is any cruelty right?), League Against Cruel Sports, 1
        July 2013 <http://www.league.org.uk/content/343/What-s-Wrong-with-
        Greyhound-Racing->

14-12   "Greyhound racing - what can you do?," League Against Cruel Sports, 1 July
        2013 <http://www.league.org.uk/content/345/What-Can-You-Do->

14-13   "Mrs Meldrew puts her foot in it with greyhound rant," Mail Online, 4 July
        2007, 1 July 2013 <http://www.dailymail.co.uk/news/article-466044/Mrs-
        Meldrew-puts-foot-greyhound-rant.html>

14-14   Crosbie, A., "Greyhounds… running for their lives," (c. 2003), Veggieglobal, 2 July 2013 <http://www.veggieglobal.com/annette-crosbie/>

14-15   "Help greyhounds," petition, (c. Dec.) 2009, number10.gov.uk

14-16   Crosbie, A., "Greyhounds need your click now," blog, 1 Dec. 2009, 4 July 2013 <http://annettecrosbie.wordpress.com/>

14-17   GE's support for the petition was based on the assumption the new regulations were "unenforceable and worthless." In defence, GE reference a press release by Local Authorities Co-ordinators of Regulatory Services in which it states: "The new legislation to be issued by DEFRA requires councils to issue licenses for greyhound tracks to operate. It does not, however, contain any offences, inviting track owners to break the law and leaving councils with no powers to prosecute them."

Local Authorities Co-ordinators of Regulatory Services, "Greyhound regulations do nothing to protect dog welfare," press release, 25 Nov. 2009

The press release was though "not best worded," according to DEFRA. If flapping tracks do not comply with the new regulations their licence can be revoked by the local authority and any track operating without a licence is committing an offence. The maximum penalties will be imprisonment for a term not exceeding six months or a fine not exceeding £5,000 or both. Alternatively, the local authority has the power to suspend a licence until such time the track can demonstrate all licensing conditions shall be met. The regulations are therefore, in theory at least, enforceable.

GE's stance in supporting the petition raises also a smile in the light of a comment expressed by Greyhounds UK as part of the consultation on new regulations: "Only licensing by local authorities of all […] premises will secure the safeguards which are needed to protect the welfare of greyhounds."

Greyhounds UK, Greyhounds UK Response, 2009, p. 1

14-18   Crosbie, A., "Promises, promises," blog, 23 Nov. 2009, 8 July 2013 <http://annettecrosbie.wordpress.com/>

14-19   "Memorandum submitted by Greyhounds UK," 24 Aug. 2004, Select Committee on Environment, Food and Rural Affairs, 8 July 2013 <http://www.publications.parliament.uk/pa/cm200405/cmselect/cmenvfru/52/4091609.htm>

14-20   Hastings, C., "RSPCA accused of political agenda over prosecution of Chipping Norton Set's hunt," Mail Online, 5 May 2012, 10 July 2013 <http://www.dailymail.co.uk/news/article-2140145/RSPCA-accused-political-agenda-prosecution-Chipping-Norton-Sets-hunt.html>

14-21   "Countryside Alliance: 'charity should lose right to call itself Royal'," Mail Online, 29 Dec. 2012, 10 July 2013 <http://www.dailymail.co.uk/news/article-2254729/RSPCA-destroys-HALF-animals-rescues--thousands-completely-healthy.html>

14-22   Royal Society for the Prevention of Cruelty to Animals, "Comments on the draft Welfare of Racing Greyhounds Regulations 2010," (c. 2009), p. 2

14-23   Royal Society for the Prevention of Cruelty to Animals, <u>RSPCA Policies on Animal Welfare</u>, revised 2010, p. 23

14-24   Royal Society for the Prevention of Cruelty to Animals, <u>The Welfare of Racing Greyhounds - RSPCA Response to the APGAW and Donoughue Reports</u>, (c. 2008), p. 7

14-25   "Memorandum submitted by Lord Lipsey, Chairman, British Greyhound Racing Board," 25 Aug. 2004, Select Committee on Environment, Food and Rural Affairs, 17 July 2013 <http://www.publications.parliament.uk/pa/cm200405/cmselect/cmenvfru/52/4091608.htm>

14-26   Monopolies and Mergers Commission, <u>Greyhound Racing: A Report on the Supply in Great Britain of the Services of Managing Greyhound Tracks</u>, July 1986, p. 57

14-27   McDowell, S., letter to Greyhound Watch, 9 Sep. 2009

        I had a number of conversations with the welfare division of Scottish Government, quizzing them on policy and highlighting the lack of track-side protection given to greyhounds under current legislation, and in response it was ultimately felt, off record so to speak, if Scotland was to adopt the Welfare of Racing Greyhounds Regulations it may result in the closure of tracks. There, I believe, lies the reason for apathy.

14-28   "Taking a gamble on better life for greyhounds," <u>Scotsman.com</u>, 25 Mar. 2008, 19 July 2013 <http://www.scotsman.com/news/taking-a-gamble-on-better-life-for-greyhounds-1-1253988>

14-29   Greig, F. (Chief Inspector, Scottish SPCA), e-mail to Sighthound Mail, 22 Sep. 2010

14-30   Royal Society for the Prevention of Cruelty to Animals, <u>The Welfare of Racing Greyhounds - RSPCA Response to the APGAW and Donoughue Reports</u>, (c. 2008), p. 2

14-31   Dogs Trust, et al., <u>Recommendations for Treatment of Greyhounds in the Animal Welfare Bill</u>, Feb. 2004, p. 3

15-1   Amphlett, F., "From the editors chair," <u>Greyhound Star</u>, Aug. 2012, p. 35

15-2   Amphlett, F., "From the editors chair," <u>Greyhound Star</u>, Sep. 2011, p. 17

15-3   Sweeney, P., "Greyhounds must have safer tracks," <u>Sporting Press</u>, 6 June 2002, 31 July 2013 <http://bgrd.co.uk/ugo/Safer%20Tracks.htm>

15-4   Amphlett, F., "From the editors chair," <u>Greyhound Star</u>, July 2012, p. 35

15-5   Royal Society for the Prevention of Cruelty to Animals, <u>The Welfare of Racing Greyhounds - RSPCA Response to the APGAW and Donoughue Reports</u>, (c. 2008), p. 3

15-6   Substances detected include: atenolol, caffeine, cocaine, cyclizine, dexamethasone, flunixin, ibuprofen, meloxicam, methylprednisolone, morphine, nandrolone, 19-norepiandrosterone, norethindrone, pholcodine, piroxicam, stanozolol and timolol.

15-7   Independent Anti-doping and Medication Control Review, Current GBGB Anti-doping and Medication Rules and their Implementation, Mar. 2010, p. 5

15-8   Kohnke, J., "Veterinary spotlight," Greyhound Star, blog, (c. 2011), 7 Aug. 2013 <http://www.greyhoundstar.net/page7/page7.html>

15-9   Kohnke, J., "The vet's clinic," Greyhound Star, May 2012, p. 9

15-10   Ross, C., "Greyhounds need homes," Salisbury Journal, 29 Aug. 2012, 8 Aug. 2013 <http://www.salisburyjournal.co.uk/news/salisbury/ salisburynews/9897905.Greyhounds_need_homes/>

15-11   British Greyhound Racing Board, Evidence for the Associate Parliamentary Group for Animal Welfare Enquiry into the Welfare of Racing Greyhounds in England, (c. 2006), p. 3

15-12   Listeners to BBC Radio Coventry and Warwickshire in June 2013 might be thinking the industry is now true to their word and open and accountable. In response to comments made on the high rate of injuries incurred by greyhounds, the promoter for Coventry Stadium, Harry Findlay, stated that he would be more than happy to give out injury figures for the above track. E-mails, however, requesting the information were ignored, and when contacted by phone (19 June 2013) Findlay stated: "If you think I am going to provide you with ammunition to try and bring us down, get fucked." It was of course just another PR stunt on the part of the industry.

15-13   Amphlett, F., "From the editors chair," Greyhound Star, Aug. 2012, p. 35

15-14   British Greyhound Racing Board, Evidence for the Associate Parliamentary Group for Animal Welfare Enquiry into the Welfare of Racing Greyhounds in England, (c. 2006), p. 9

15-15   "The final flutter," The Economist, 9 Feb. 2013, 15 Aug. 2013 <http://www. economist.com/news/britain/21571462-changes-gambling-habits-may-kill-dog-racing-good-final-flutter>

15-16   This section of the Act covers England and Wales. Similar legislation exists in Scotland under the Animal Health and Welfare (Scotland) Act 2006, Section 24, and for Northern Ireland under the Welfare of Animals Act (Northern Ireland) 2011, Section 9.

15-17   Department for Environment, Food and Rural Affairs, Summary of Responses to the Consultation on the Welfare of Racing Greyhounds Regulations 2010 from 30 April 2009 to 22 July 2009, Oct. 2009, p. 49

15-18   May, L., "Businessman Paschal Taggart unveils plan to turn Wimbledon stadium into 'Royal Ascot' of dog racing," Your Local Guardian, 1 Mar. 2013, 23 Aug. 2013 <http://www.yourlocalguardian.co.uk/news/local/ topstories/10261660.Multi_million_pound_plan_to_turn_stadium_into__ Royal_Ascot__of_dog_racing/>

Abbreviations

AFG	Action for Greyhounds
APGAW	Associate Parliamentary Group for Animal Welfare
APPGG	All Party Parliamentary Greyhound Group
BAGS	Bookmakers Afternoon Greyhound Service
BGRB	British Greyhound Racing Board
BGRF	British Greyhound Racing Fund
BVOF	Belle Vue Owners Forum
CSPCA	Cork Society for the Prevention of Cruelty to Animals
DEFRA	Department for Environment, Food and Rural Affairs
DIS	finished at distance
DNF	did not finish
DOA	dead on arrival
DOB	date of birth
DSPCA	Dublin Society for the Prevention of Cruelty to Animals
GA	Greyhound Action
GBGB	Greyhound Board of Great Britain
GE	Greyt Exploitations
GOBATA	Greyhound Owners, Breeders and Trainers Association
GRA	Greyhound Racing Association
GRW	Greyhound Rescue Wales
GRWE	Greyhound Rescue West of England
G4U	Greyhounds 4 U
ICC	Irish Coursing Club
IGB	Irish Greyhound Board
ISPCA	Irish Society for the Prevention of Cruelty to Animals
LA	local authority
LACS	League Against Cruel Sports
NCC	National Coursing Club
NGRC	National Greyhound Racing Club
NGRS	National Greyhound Racing Society

PTS	put to sleep
RCPA	Racecourse Promoters Association
RGT	Retired Greyhound Trust
RSPCA	Royal Society for the Prevention of Cruelty to Animals
RVC	Royal Veterinary College
SDBV	Shut Down Belle Vue
SGV	Society of Greyhound Veterinarians
SSPCA	Scottish Society for the Prevention of Cruelty to Animals
URL	uniform resource locator
USPCA	Ulster Society for the Prevention of Cruelty to Animals
UKAS	United Kingdom Accreditation Service
WSPCA	Waterford Society for the Prevention of Cruelty to Animals

Greyhound colour/sex abbreviations

bd	brindle
be	blue
bk	black
f	fawn
w	white
dk	dark
lt	light
b	female (bitch)
d	male (dog)

Race classification abbreviations

A	standard 4 bends
D	dash 2 bends
H	hurdle
HP	handicapped
M	marathon 8 bends
OR	open
S	stayer 6 bends

Greyhounds featured in AFG calendars and given mention on page 62. Above: On the Dot. Below: No Way Jose. Following page: Slieve Gallen